LOTUS
Twin-Cam Engine

LOTUS
Twin-Cam Engine

A comprehensive guide to the design,

development, restoration and maintenance

of the Lotus-Ford twin-cam engine

Miles Wilkins

Published in 1988 by Osprey Publishing Limited
27A Floral Street, London WC2E 9DP
Member company of the George Philip Group

Sole distributors for the USA

Osceola, Wisconsin 54020, USA

British Library Cataloguing in Publication Data

Wilkins, Miles
    Lotus twin-cam engine.
    1. Cars. Twin-cam engines, to 1980
    I. Title
    629.2'5
ISBN 0-85045-676-2

Editor Tony Thacker
Design Gwyn Lewis

Filmset by Tameside Filmsetting Ltd,
Ashton-under-Lyne, Lancashire

Printed by BAS Printers Ltd, Over Wallop,
Hampshire, Great Britain

While great care is taken to ensure that the information in this book is accurate, neither the author, editor nor publisher can accept any liability for loss, damage or injury caused by errors in or omissions from the information given.

Page 2
A unique picture of John Miles in his twin-cam engined Elan 26R, at the Montes Claros circuit near Lisbon, in Portugal, in 1966. He came second overall to a Ferrari 250LM. Note, also, the locally registered 'road' Elan S2 behind him

Contents

Acknowledgements

I am deeply indebted to the following people, without whom this record of the Lotus twin-cam engine would not have been possible. In particular, I am grateful to the three men who gave me a continuous history: the late Roy Badcock, whose tragic death left a void in Lotus history—I shall not forget the time he gave me while struggling to keep his illness at bay; Steve Sanville who, as production engineer, followed the engine from its inception; and Bob Dance who gave me much valuable information from his personal diaries.

Also thanks to Graham Atkin, who gave me so much on the Federal engines, and to Tony Rudd who, of course, did so much work with the engine as well. To my wife Belinda, for taking the bulk of the photographs, and encouraging me to write when I did not want to; to Ian Symms of Fibreglass Services for assisting with all the practical aspects; and to Dilys Simmons for typing the manuscript. To Lotus for allowing me to reproduce drawings and specifications, and especially to Roy Smith, Hugh Wilson, Colin Gethin, John Bloomfield, Clive Roberts, Peter Brand, Joe Wopetisch, and Mike Pomfret. To Ford Motor Co. Ltd, for its help, and particularly to Steve Clark and Sheila Knapman at the Picture Library at Aveley, for their kindness in allowing me to sift through hundreds of photographs. At Boreham, the Ford Motorsport headquarters, to Peter Ashcroft and Bill Meade for their rally experiences. To Graham Nearn and David Wakefield of Caterham Car Sales. To Mike Costin at Cosworth, Richard Ansdale and to ex-Lotus personalities, Brian Luff, Roy McGregor, Graham Arnold, Colin Gane, Mike Warner; to Andrew Ferguson of Lotus Marketing and to Fred Bushell. To John Miles for his exploits in the Elan and 47s. To Peter Day of Daytune, Pat Thomas of Kelvedon Motors, Anthony Mantle of Climax Engine Services, George Robinson of Vegantune, Ian Walker of Blue Flash Products, and Chris Walters of Chris Walters Engineering Ltd, for all their help in providing information. To Vincent Hayden for his brochures, and to *Autocar* for allowing me to reproduce the Harry Mundy article, and to Roger Dunbar of the Elva Owners Club.

Finally, my thanks to all those to whom I spoke on the telephone and have forgotten to mention, to those who sent in photographs, and, with apologies, to Doug Nye and Jabby Crombac for rewriting some of their misplaced 'facts' in their *Story of Lotus 1961–71* and *Colin Chapman, The Man and His Cars* respectively. And to Graham Robson who put all this into shape, my unbounded gratitude.

Introduction

It is my sincere wish that this book will become the standard reference work for the famous Lotus twin-cam engine. In compiling it, I hope to put a stop to all the inaccurate comments still being written about the engine.

In the course of researching material for the book, the overriding comments I received—where people's memories could be trusted—were that things were often done, at the time, which could not possibly be done today, and that certain things were done to help the sales departments, rather than for purely technical reasons.

During its career the engine attracted several larger-than-life characters, not least Colin Chapman himself, Harry Mundy and Keith Duckworth. Certain people seemed to attract more credit than they deserved for their involvement in the engine's development than was ultimately justified by events. This becomes evident when the reader studies the text. In particular, I am sorry that Harry Mundy was not willing to relate his experiences, and his involvement, in the project. .

The book is divided into three parts, covering the engine's entire production life, the process of stripping and rebuilding an engine, and a comprehensive guide to specifications and production data.

Miles Wilkins
January 1988

PART ONE

Development of the twin-cam

1 The concept

Why did Colin Chapman choose Ford? There were several reasons: something had to be done about the spiralling cost of the Elite, with its Coventry Climax Type FWE engine, which required regular rebuilds (new bearings every 30–35,000 miles, for instance), was extremely costly, and of which supplies were limited. After all, in the first place it was Colin who had persuaded Leonard Lee, chairman of Coventry Climax, to produce 1000 engines against his will, as Coventry Climax was really a racing-engine manufacturer (FWA, FPF twin-cam, and later the $1\frac{1}{2}$-litre V8), not production road-engine builders. Lotus' proposed new car (the Elan) could not be allowed to suffer these problems.

Colin had originally met Ford's Walter Hayes when the latter was editor of the *Sunday Dispatch* and had asked him to write a motoring column (in the end, it was ghosted for Colin). This initial meeting bore fruit later when Hayes became Ford's Public Relations chief, and they discussed the possible use of Ford engines. Eventually, a deal was struck, for the Elan and what we now know as the Lotus-Cortina.

Ford had a new long-term engine strategy (unlike BMC, who seemed to have none at all), with modern tooling which could be adapted to the building of many different four-cylinder engines—these included the 105E, 109E, 113E and the 116E derivatives. Hayes outlined the prospects to Colin, and it was quite clear that there was potential for development.

The way to go, Chapman thought, was to use the bottom end from a standard engine (which would be cheap!), but to discard the standard cylinder head, since this was not likely to produce enough power for his purposes. Prior to this discussion, Colin had owned a Ford Consul, the

Above
Colin Chapman, inspiration behind the twin-cam engine. This picture was taken only a few months before his untimely death

Right and overleaf
An important early description of the twin-cam engine—important because the article was written by Autocar's *Harry Mundy, who had conceived the engine in the first place! Note that the engine illustrated had the central cam-cover nuts, which were not used on production versions. The distributor is an early 25D4 type, and the inlet tracts are of the 'long' type. Courtesy Autocar*

Lotus-Engine Builders

TWIN O.H.C. CONVERSION ON FORD 105E/109E ENGINES FOR SPORTS CAR USE

The new 1·5-litre engine installed in a Lotus 23 and which made its début in the Nürburgring 1000 Kilometres race

IT is the ambition of most manufacturers, whether they be small or large, to be self-contained provided it makes economic sense. In this way, they can be independent of outside suppliers and their design can be more flexible. Colin Chapman, head of Lotus, has always wanted to add an engine section to his present organization; not to build Grand Prix engines but to manufacture power units, at first in part, for his wide range of sports cars. Of course, a plant for complete production would be impossible for such a small organization; therefore, his first effort in this field is a twin overhead camshaft conversion based on the Ford 105E/109E engines. It is suitable for either the 997 c.c. Anglia or the 1,340 c.c. Classic unit in standard form, but the first experimental type, which competed in the Nürburgring 1000 Kilometres race last Sunday, was one of the latter engines enlarged to 1·5-litres.

Naturally, the economics of such a task depend upon using as many standard items as possible and, broadly, a production Ford cylinder block with crankshaft, con-rods, pistons, camshaft and drives for the oil pump and distributor are retained; the standard head assembly and front cover, including the water pump casing, are discarded. To pick up existing locations such as cylinder head bolt centres, water passages and auxiliary drives, demands compromises. For example, Ford use graded pistons which can mean slight variations—only a matter of a few ten-thousandths of an inch—between the skirt diameters of an engine set, so that it was necessary to retain the standard flat top pistons already fitted to a particular block; otherwise a wide range of substitute types would need to be held in stock to suit the graded cylinder bores.

The use of flat top pistons in an engine of considerably over-square proportions presented a problem in attaining a high compression ratio with a segmental spherical head using opposed valves. As a result the angle of the valves, disposed equally at 27 deg to the vertical, is rather narrow; also, the circular form of the combustion chamber on the joint face is 2·50in. dia. and thus slightly overlaps the bore of 3·187in. This is something of an advantage, for it promotes squish which, in conjunction with tangental entry inlet ports provides turbulent combustion. Sparking plugs, long reach 14mm dia., are placed vertically in the combustion chamber and off-set 0·87in. from the cylinder centre.

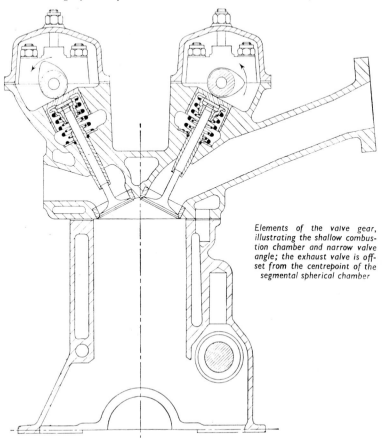

Elements of the valve gear, illustrating the shallow combustion chamber and narrow valve angle; the exhaust valve is off-set from the centrepoint of the segmental spherical chamber

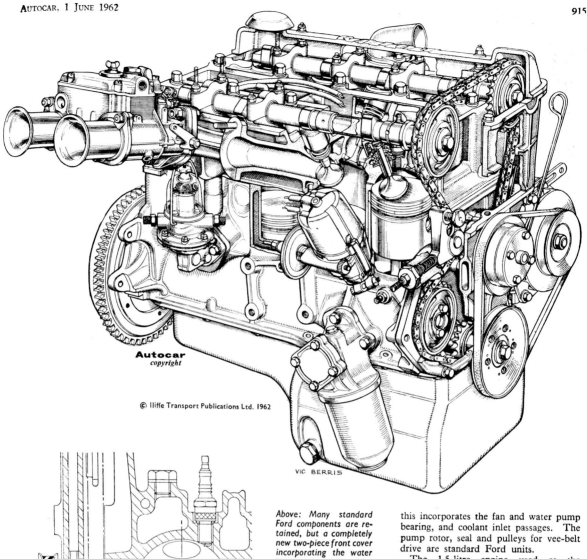

Autocar
copyright

© Iliffe Transport Publications Ltd. 1962

VIC BERRIS

Above: Many standard Ford components are retained, but a completely new two-piece front cover incorporating the water pump passages was necessary. The standard Ford firing order of 1-2-4-3 has been changed to the more orthodox 1-3-4-2

Left: Longitudinal section of the coolant pump and the first cylinder. A flexible nylon block ensures an adequate seal between the coolant passages and the timing chest

Valve operation is by inverted, bucket-type tappets with varying thickness biscuits to set the valve clearance. Tappets operate directly in the aluminium head and enclose the duplex valve springs. Each camshaft is supported in four bearings, the end cam on each shaft being overhung. This was necessary to avoid existing holding-down studs, but in conjunction with the large diameter shaft it has proved quite satisfactory. Each camshaft is drilled from end to end, a pressure feed being taken from the main oil system to the front bearing and thus through the hollow shaft to the other three.

The standard Ford camshaft and its sprocket are retained to drive the oil pump and distributor, but naturally the tappets are removed. Two more standard Ford sprockets are used for each of the new Lotus camshafts. The drive is a one-stage single roller chain, with a spring-loaded jockey sprocket having an external screw adjustment on the slack side; a rubber-faced block on the tight side prevents chain thrash. To enclose this extended chain drive and match-up with the front tunnel in the cylinder head, a new two-piece timing cover was necessary on the cylinder block. The front portion of

this incorporates the fan and water pump bearing, and coolant inlet passages. The pump rotor, seal and pulleys for vee-belt drive are standard Ford units.

The 1.5-litre engine used at the Nürburgring is not a highly tuned racing unit. It has relatively mild valve timing with opening periods of 248 deg for the inlet and exhaust valves in conjunction with 30 deg overlap at T.D.C. Inlet valve throat diameter is 1·30in. and the exhaust 1·20in., with head diameters of 1·53in. and 1·45in. respectively. Mixture is supplied by two twin-choke Weber carburettors mounted directly on the extended inlet ports formed integrally in the head. In this form, and with a compression ratio of 9·3 to 1, the engine develops 104 b.h.p. at 5,900 r.p.m. Using the same head assembly on a 1,340 c.c. engine, and consequently a lower compression ratio of 8·4 to 1, produced a power output of 87 b.h.p. at 5,500 r.p.m.

Naturally, more highly tuned engines are under development for competition purposes to give considerably more power than those quoted above. One such unit, using the 997 c.c. Anglia base, will be used in the Le Mans 24 Hours race, but no power outputs can be released at present.

Finally, these conversions are only in the development stage and thus at present not available from the company for sale to private customers. **H. M**

12

engine of which had a Raymond Mays cylinder head, and which gave a great deal of power ('It nearly killed me!' Mike Costin remembers), and he was sufficiently impressed by this to realize that a different head could be placed on the Ford block to make a more powerful engine.

Therefore, Colin approached Harry Mundy (then technical editor of *Autocar*, but ex-chief designer at Coventry-Climax, who would later take over engine design at Jaguar). Harry often used to pop into Lotus, to look at the latest developments at Hornsey and Cheshunt—now he was asked to act as a consultant and design a new head for the Ford block.

Early in 1961, Harry Mundy designed the twin-cam cylinder head, working out all the valve angles, the layout of the combustion chamber, the porting, the inlet tracts, and the geometry of the camshafts. At this stage, however, the design was only 'in the rough'. Stories of Colin's offer to Mundy—'I'll give you a £1 royalty for every engine we build, or a cash sum'—are well known. Presumably, Mundy did not think that many engines would be produced, as he took a cash sum, reputed to be £1000.

The detailed design work was carried out, in the summer of 1961, by Richard Ansdale who, at the time, was a transmission designer at Thorneycroft. He had known Colin since 1956

and had helped out with the design of the infamous Lotus 12 gearbox (or 'queerbox', as it became known!). Later, he joined Plessey as assistant chief designer.

Richard was responsible for translating the basic rough drawings into a workable, practical design, and he was totally responsible for drawing the water-pump arrangement, front cover, and backplate—for the twin-cam head overhung the Ford block at the front. The water pump employed the Ford 105E bearing, but the impellor and seal housings were new.

Like Mundy, Ansdale acted as consultant to Lotus. He never actually worked at Cheshunt, and took only a pittance for the work: 'I enjoyed doing it, out of friendship to Colin, and I wanted the project to succeed.' In fact, although Mundy has often been given credit for the design, Richard Ansdale really did more work to make the project viable and practical. (Richard still has the original drawings, but sadly these are now too faint to reproduce here.)

After producing the drawings, Richard did no more work on the engine design, and the task of turning it into reality fell on Steve Sanville, who

Section through the twin-cam cylinder head, showing the various angles, as originally schemed by Harry Mundy

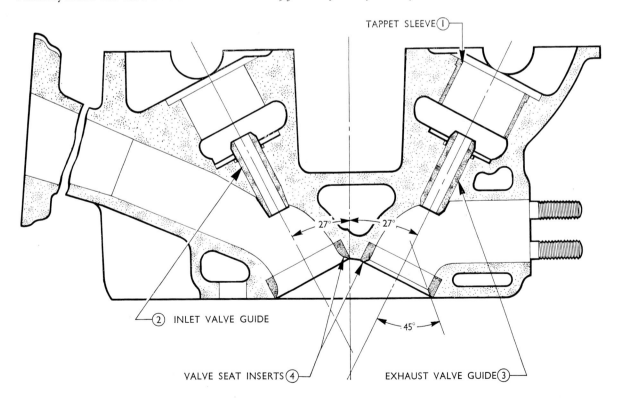

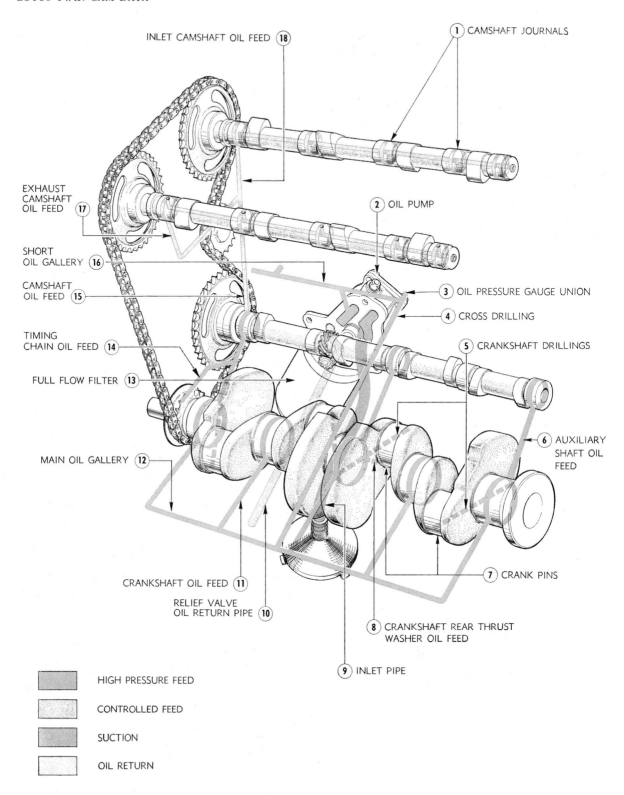

INLET CAMSHAFT OIL FEED ⑱

① CAMSHAFT JOURNALS

EXHAUST CAMSHAFT OIL FEED ⑰

② OIL PUMP

SHORT OIL GALLERY ⑯

③ OIL PRESSURE GAUGE UNION

CAMSHAFT OIL FEED ⑮

④ CROSS DRILLING

TIMING CHAIN OIL FEED ⑭

⑤ CRANKSHAFT DRILLINGS

FULL FLOW FILTER ⑬

⑥ AUXILIARY SHAFT OIL FEED

MAIN OIL GALLERY ⑫

⑦ CRANK PINS

CRANKSHAFT OIL FEED ⑪

RELIEF VALVE OIL RETURN PIPE ⑩

⑧ CRANKSHAFT REAR THRUST WASHER OIL FEED

⑨ INLET PIPE

HIGH PRESSURE FEED

CONTROLLED FEED

SUCTION

OIL RETURN

The standard engine's lubrication system. This particular car has a four-bolt crankshaft, with appropriate oil pick-up strainer

had joined Lotus in 1957 to work in the engine shop (alongside Graham Hill), carrying out basic modifications to Coventry Climax engines and MGA close-ratio gearboxes—and trying to get the Lotus 12 'queerbox' to work properly.

As early as 1958, Steve remembers talking to Colin about the possibilities of various engines, and even then the Raymond Mays cylinder-head conversion for the Consul engine set him thinking. With the twin-cam, he was responsible for setting all production tolerances and personally took the drawings along to Percey Smith (in Goswell Road, London EC1) to have the original casting pattern made. Unfortunately, the pattern was left over a blisteringly-hot Bank Holiday weekend and became warped, due to the excessive heat build-up in the shed in which it was kept! This resulted in awful castings being produced, until someone realized what had happened, and they had new patterns made. While all this was going on, Ford introduced the 1340 cc 109E engine for their Classic/Capri range, and this formed the basis for the whole concept of the Lotus twin-cam engine.

Bob Dance (now Lotus F1 senior chief mechanic) joined Lotus on 18 August 1961, essentially as a gearbox man, but he was placed in the engine shop with Neil Francis from New Zealand. Steve Sanville was foreman. At this time, the twin-cam engine project was known as M2E (Lotus project numbers are prefixed by 'M' even today), and the Elan project as M2.

The initial step was taken on 6 September 1961 when Bob stripped a 109E engine for evaluation. A test-bed for the 'new' engine was completed by mid-September and, at the end of the month, the front cover (cast by Birmid) was fitted to the block together with the three-bearing crankshaft and the jackshaft. Work was halted then until an experimental twin-camshaft head arrived (also cast by Birmid).

The engine's timing could be altered by using a vernier sprocket on each camshaft. The latter had already been drawn geometrically by Harry Mundy, and detailed by Ron Burr (now at Jaguar), at Coventry Climax, for it carried the profile of the standard, three-bearing, ET418 cam used in the FWE Elite engine. After final assembly, the very first Lotus twin-cam engine ran on 10 October 1961.

On 12 October the engine ran continuously for two hours and, when it was stripped down, all seemed to be well. On 16 October power tests were conducted—no record of the results exists, but the power is said to have been around 85 bhp. On 26 October the engine was stripped, and the head was installed on an 1100 cc 105E block fitted with the 109E crank and pistons (which were milled 0.030 in. below the block face). This engine was first run on 1 November, but the timing slipped; it was rebuilt and run again a week later. Meanwhile, an engine mock-up was made to try out in the first prototype Elan. Also, instead of Webers, a single $1\frac{1}{2}$ in. SU carburettor was tried, followed by two $1\frac{1}{4}$ in. SUs, all on the original (only) head. A $1\frac{3}{4}$ in. SU was tried when the second head arrived, but it was all to no avail, and the Webers were reinstated. One problem which manifested itself time and time again was cylinder-head gasket failure. The first time it happened was when the engine was running on the single $1\frac{3}{4}$ in. SU carburettor.

By the end of November 1961, a second 1100 cc engine was running, and during power tests this gave between 85 and 90 bhp. Christmas 1961 saw the first engine break its crankshaft (too much power for the three-bearing bottom end) at 4500 rpm, while the second engine also broke its cam followers (tappets), so for a time the entire twin-cam project was halted, for lack of usable engines.

A third 109E engine was acquired and stripped for enlargement to 1500 cc (actually 1477 cc). After modification, it was assembled, together with the second 1100 cc unit (now using a 1340 cc 109E block). This second unit blew its head gasket again and also ran its bearings. A change from Glacier to Vandervell bearings resulted in no more bearing failures due to the use of lead/indium in the surface overlay (see later).

On 18 January 1962 the engine-development vehicle was prepared. This was a left-hand-drive Ford Anglia (335 AXY), purchased from the Belgian Embassy—it had to be lhd because the rear Weber carburettor would foul the rhd master cylinders at this stage! Bob Dance and Steve Sanville fitted a 4.1:1 differential, uprated the front suspension and installed disc brakes. Then the third engine was winched in. The twin-cam Anglia took to the road for the very first time during the first weekend of February 1962, and immediately covered 400 miles without a hitch.

With all this activity going on, normal life at Cheshunt was continuing. Elites were still being built and sold, together with the Sevens and formula and sports racing cars. Mike Costin, who was still at Cheshunt fulfilling his contract as

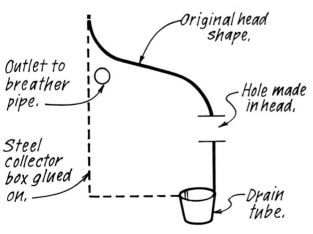

Above
Early days at Cheshunt. At this time, the Essex Racing Team was using Lotus 235, fitted with 1498 cc twin-cam engines. Left to right: Trevor Taylor, two Essex Team mechanics, Jim Clark, and Bob Dance

Left
The velocity-drop chamber

technical director, left in late 1962 to join Keith Duckworth at Cosworth Engineering, which he had formed with Keith to develop race engines—'I stayed on because I had a wife, and Colin gave me a salary and a company car . . . Keith had a little money of his own and therefore was not as financially tied as I was!' Mike remembers flying down to see Harry Weslake, at Rye in Sussex, to give him the first head for evaluation and gas flowing—this was carried out with only minor alterations to the original design, and the first engine (now enlarged to 1477 cc) was fitted in the Anglia in place of the third. Amazingly, Steve Sanville then took the Anglia, with a second engine in the back, to Weber at Bologna in Italy, for carburettor evaluation. The engine survived the ten-day trip. While Steve was away, the first journal to be allowed a secret look at the new twin-cam engine was *Motoring News* on 28 February 1962.

Meanwhile, it was realized that someone would have to assemble the engines when production began in earnest, and rather than tackle this at Cheshunt, which at the time could not cope because of a lack of machinery, time and finance (the Elite was costing Lotus a fortune, and because of its very high asking price—over £2000—it was not selling), several firms were approached. J. A. Prestwich, manufacturers of JAP motorcycle engines, in Tottenham, North London, agreed to do it, and on 13 March the third engine was delivered to them for inspection. Unfortunately, when it came back, its crankshaft broke.

In the meantime, the Anglia was still doing sterling service (eventually over 20,000 miles of engine testing were carried out), but by this time oil was plastering everything in sight, since it was being pumped out of the breather. To cope with this problem, Steve designed a velocity-drop chamber where the oil could expand, lose its pressure and drain away. Bob Dance glued on a fabricated, steel, corner-piece chamber, and led a tube from this to the original breather vent in the block to act as a drain. The modification was added to all subsequent prototype head castings. Eventually, it was cast into the production heads and no further alteration was made, so a very simple idea stayed to the end!

The next major development occurred in May 1962 when Ford announced their new 1500 (actually 1498 cc) 116E block with its five-bearing crankshaft. Colin Chapman, Steve Sanville and

John Standen (chief buyer) lost no time in visiting Ford at Aveley and returning with a 1500 block in the boot of their car. On 14 May the very first prototype 1498 cc five-bearing twin-cam was assembled, using the fourth head, and promptly blew its head gasket. The engine was hastily rebuilt, together with a spare (1477 cc), and a week later Bob left Cheshunt to take a Lotus 23, complete with the first 1498 cc twin-cam, to the 1000-km race at the Nürburgring. He had finished building the car on 24 May, and Jim Clark and Trevor Taylor practised with it the next day. In the race on Sunday 26 May, history was written by Jim as he outpaced everyone, until he went off the road, overcome by fumes from a fractured exhaust pipe, having led for 12 laps. The official race debut of the Lotus twin-cam had caused a sensation.

Back at Cheshunt, a second 116E block had arrived, and this was duly winched into the Anglia in place of the long-suffering 1477 cc unit. The continuing problem was still that of blowing head gaskets, and Coopers developed a special material in an effort to provide a seal between the cast-iron block and aluminium head—this material helped for a while. In July a fourth 1498 cc engine was assembled, but it still had gasket problems. However, with a new gasket, an air box and exhaust system it was ready for use in the second Elan prototype. Throughout August development continued on this engine with regard to valve timing and carburettor settings.

During the next few weeks, the pressure really built up, since the 1962 Motor Show was looming up and in true Lotus fashion there was still no car ready. Furthermore, the Ford Lotus-Cortina programme had yet to begin in earnest. This project had been the culmination of the meeting between Colin and Walter Hayes, during which Colin outlined the twin-cam engine project, and Walter explained that his task was to promote the Ford image, with a view to increasing sales into the younger market sector. It seemed obvious that the new engine, together with a suitable package, would enhance the Consul Cortina (the Consul name was dropped later), which was to sell in 1200 (1198 cc) form. Walter Hayes offered the deal, whereby Colin could redesign the rear suspension (to coil springs and the famous A-frame, instead of leaf springs), fit the engine and assemble the whole car at Cheshunt. Needless to say, the package was accepted and with it came (eventually) some much needed finance.

Le Mans 1962, with Mike Costin at the wheel of the Lotus 23. This was the year in which the scrutineers banned the car from racing because of its different stud fixing arrangements for the front and rear wheels. As a result of this fracas, Colin Chapman vowed that he would never again enter cars for the French 24-hour race. The full-width screen was made necessary by particular race regulations in that year. This car did not have a twin-cam engine at the time, but one had been scheduled to be fitted

After that everything seemed to happen at once. To keep events in chronological order is difficult, since there were really two engine programmes—for the Cortina and for the Elan—albeit culminating in a common goal.

As of August 1962, no production engine had yet been built, although two Lotus 23s were fitted with 1498 cc units. These engines came from Keith Duckworth, who was based at Edmonton in North London, where he and Mike Costin had founded Cosworth Engineering. Since July Duckworth had been playing with porting and camshafts. (He drew up the S/E cam.)

With a potential racing programme for 1600 cc cars, Ford realized that the 116E block could be stretched to this size (and ultimately beyond), and Colin thought that he might as well have a 1600 cc engine for his Elan, too. So Keith Duckworth was also given the opportunity of developing the Lotus-Cortina engine for Group 2 racing. He redesigned the top end (after Mundy, Ansdale and Weslake!) to make it both a real racer and suitable for production engines. Therefore, the final shape of the head, including the oil-breather arrangement, was produced by Keith Duckworth.

By now Mike Costin, free from his contract with Lotus, had joined Keith—he was instrumental in smoothing the way between Keith and Colin (they liked each other, but . . .) for this contract. (In that year Cosworth built 125 Formula Junior engines—an amazing feat.)

Meanwhile, the first Consul Cortina had arrived secretly and was under wraps at Cheshunt. It had a standard bodyshell—the alloy panels and unique paint scheme of Ermine white with a Lotus green flash came later for production cars. So during August Bob and Steve winched in a 1498 cc twin-cam for trial, but it soon became apparent that it would not fit. Because of the length of the inlet tracts, the Webers fouled the inner wings, so in a highly empiric manner Bob cut the ends of the tracts to the requisite length with a hacksaw.

At about this time Neil Francis decided he had had enough and left, his place being taken by Colin Gane (who stayed at Hethel until 1975—he is still with Steve Sanville at Norvic Racing Engines. Steve left Hethel in 1969 to start his own business). Bob also had a young helper from Farnborough who had come to gain practical experience, but he did not last long—his name was Robin Herd who, in time, was to set up March. Eventually, Bob left for March in 1969, partly because of this early encounter, but he returned to Lotus in 1971 and has stayed there ever since.

Meanwhile, Jim Clark was frightening himself silly with the ultimate Q-car, the dear old Anglia. One memorable run occurred after a Goodwood meeting when he broke all records on his journey back home to Duns in Scotland.

With the Motor Show only two weeks away, the Cortina was undergoing trials and the Elan engine had just blown yet another head gasket on the test-bed. On 11 October Bob and Steve went to J. A. Prestwich with the contract for building the production 1498 cc engines. After protracted debates, the first engine appeared for testing (one of the points debated was that JAP wanted to do all their own testing on compressed air, which was not at all the same as running on fuel—Lotus requested they test all their engines on the latter!).

On 21 October 1962 the first production engine ran, but it gave only 85 bhp. Obviously, this was useless. After a quick strip-down, more fettling of ports, and ignition changes, the engine still did not perform properly (later it was found that number four piston was seizing in its bore as the temperature rose), but after a mild panic, the Elan 1500 actually made it to the Motor Show with a pre-production 1498 cc unit in it. In true Lotus fashion, it was hardly finished, as Mike Warner (inspector at the time, who later ran Lotus Components until 1971, dealing with, among other things, the Lotus Sevens) recalls, 'We were up all night, and the headlights were propped up on springs and pieces of wood!'

At that point the Elan could not run. But, as usual with all new Lotus models, it caused a sensation, and a flood of orders followed. Unfortunately, nobody had any cars to sell, least of all Lotus themselves!

After the Motor Show, Bob Dance arrived at MIRA, near Nuneaton, to conduct fuel-

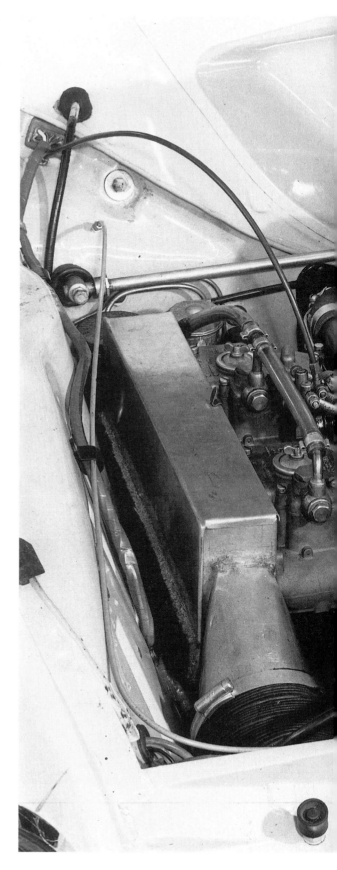

This is a very rare photograph of one of the first experimental Lotus-Cortinas. It was taken at Cheshunt in January 1963. Note the prototype oil-filler-cum-breather cap on the inlet side of the cam cover. The cover was not yet in its final form, for it was more rounded at the front. On this engine, inlet tracts were bolted to the head, not cast integrally. This was a Birmid sand-cast head—later engines had William Mills die-cast heads. Note, too, that the carburettor air box is a prototype fabricated item

consumption tests, which were extremely promising. By November 1962 another $1\frac{1}{8}$ in. had been removed from the length of the inlet tracts—scientifically this time—so that an air box could be fitted (the first reduction in length only allowed the Webers to fit), the flanges were then glued back on and reinforced with fibreglass. This was the inlet-tract length that would persist for the entire production run. The engines were now being tested at Cosworth, because the Cheshunt test-bed could not supply enough water.

Throughout December 1962 endurance tests were run, and peak power was raised to 96.2 bhp at 5500 rpm. By this time, the Elan head had been doctored to allow the fitting of an air-box system; but panic was setting in, for the Lotus-Cortina was due to be launched at the Racing Car Show in January 1963, and the Elan should have been selling already. Available finance was almost non-existent, and everything looked very gloomy indeed. However, the final development of the concept occurred at the end of November 1962 with the arrival of the graded 1558 cc 116E blocks; by the middle of December, Steve and his team were at last producing the 1558 cc twin-cam engines.

In January the new Lotus-Cortina was announced at the Racing Car Show, complete with its 1558 cc engine. Once again, here was a sensation which turned into a nightmare, because of delayed production (1000 had to be built to achieve homologation), and eventually the Lotus-Cortina could only race towards the end of 1963 under the Saloon and GT banner. At the time, Ford were most unhappy.

The Lotus-Cortina was announced to the world's press in Monte Carlo on 21 January 1963. During that month a new engine was assembled with an inlet tract cast integrally with the head (by Birmid) and the latest production-specification camshafts utilizing Keith Duckworth's CPL1 and CPL2 (Cosworth Production Lotus 1 and 2) profiles. CPL1 was S/E specification (0.349 in. lift), i.e. with 22/62/62/22 timing, and CPL2 was a higher lift cam with 26/66/66/26 timing, giving approximately 140 bhp. The engines were now being run for 11 hours continuously, but even at this late stage they were still suffering repeated head-gasket failures. Therefore, one of the 'new' heads was fitted to the Anglia, which was press-ganged into yet more development work.

A historic moment came in January 1963 when the first two production Elan 1600s were finished.

Above
The very first cut-away drawing of a Lotus-Cortina, completed in 1962 before the car was launched

Below right
Early Lotus-Cortinas, of 1963, still retained the 'Consul' name badge on the bonnet

In the middle of February, JAP installed their own Heenan & Froud dynamometer for all twin-cam testing, and the first 1558 cc engine they tested gave 97 bhp; the situation could only get better, since the 1498 cc engine eventually produced 100 bhp at 5500 rpm.

As they entered 1963, things were grim at Lotus, with no cars to sell, dealers getting upset, Ford applying pressure, head-gasket problems still occuring, even on production cars, and everything being done in a hurry. The old Elite was not selling, but in an effort to salvage something for the company and its dealers, more bodies (about 50) were ordered from Bristol Aircraft Company by Fred Bushell—Colin's accountant since 1953 and life-long right-hand

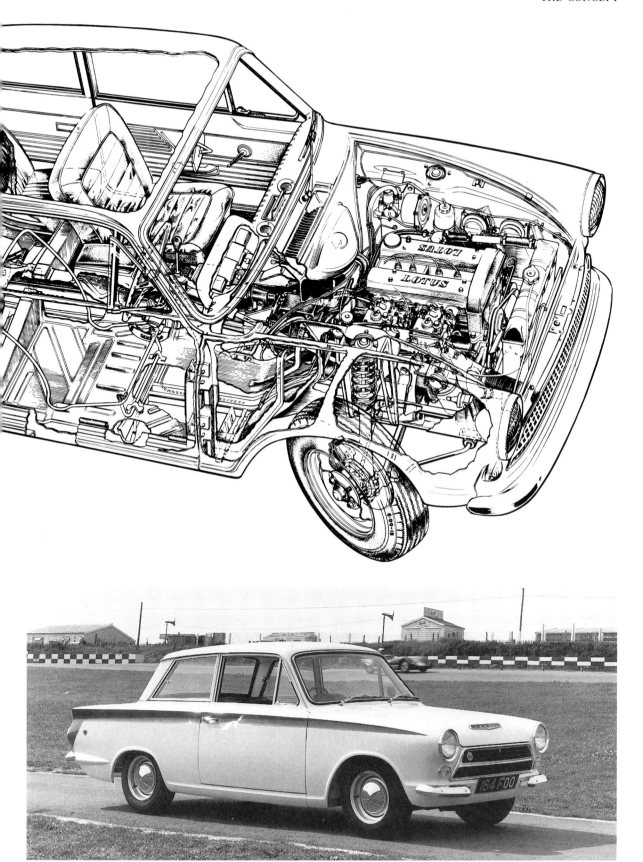

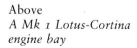

Above
*A Mk 1 Lotus-Cortina
engine bay*

Right
*A Lotus Elan S1 engine
bay, showing that the
cam-cover and engine-bay
colours are both incorrect*

man. Even this project was cancelled after the bodies arrived at Cheshunt, and few were ever built into cars.

However, there were a few lighthearted moments, one such being when Bob Dance placed a frog in the test-bed water tank after an intended practical joke was not played and the frog had to be kept alive. Unfortunately, he forgot it was there until there was an almighty explosion. Steve Sanville read the Riot Act, and after the fuss had died down Bob discovered, to his horror, the remains of the frog strewn all over the place; it had got stuck in the supply pipe, starving the engine of water, and a blow-up was inevitable.

The atmosphere at Lotus, both at Hornsey and Cheshunt (and even today at Hethel) was always convivial, free and easy, and things were done that could never be carried out today, like sawing off inlet tracts! It was against this background that everyone wished the projects to succeed and ultimately gave their all for Colin, rightly or wrongly. As Bob said, 'We had a good time!'

2 Early production experiences

Only 11 1498 cc production engines were ever made—six being fitted in 23s, and five in Elans. These were only intended for development work (and Jim Clark used one of the 1500 cc Elans), so do not believe stories put about by certain people (later employed by Lotus, but who were not there at the time) that 20-plus were made, and that all were recalled because Colin Chapman wanted the 1498 cc engine for his sports racers, i.e. the 23s. This was untrue since, as Steve Sanville has pointed out, as soon as the 1600 engine was produced by Ford, the Elan was to benefit, and the 23 became the 23B with the 1600 unit in it (1558 and 1594 cc).

Prior to JAP formally taking on the production contract, the heads were sand-cast by Birmid (Birmingham Aluminium at Smethwick) but were unsatisfactory. At the time William Mills (at Wednesbury in Staffordshire) were trying to develop die-casting as an addition to their established sand-casting business, which included producing heads for Jaguar. They submitted an amazingly low quote of £2000 for patterns. The next lowest received by Lotus was in the region of £10,000, so, needless to say, Colin gave them the job.

JAP's task was to machine the heads and assemble them and then to fit them on to the built-up blocks from Dagenham. The first engine with a die-cast head arrived at Cheshunt on 21 February 1963 and promptly leaked water everywhere. A second die-cast head was used on 25 February with better results. Now, at least, the engine was beginning to be produced, although the rejection rate for heads was still incredibly high (up to eight out of ten at one time).

The die-cast saga continued until Lotus thought that enough was enough, and Steve

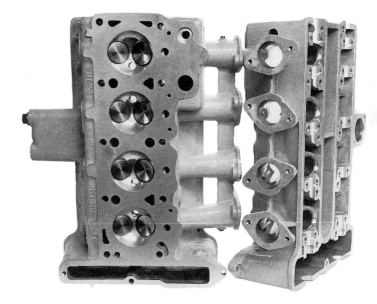

At the right of this display is a completely bare Weber cylinder head before being studded or fitted with valve guides and seats. To the left is a head with valves in place. 'WM' on the head casting means that it was produced by William Mills, while the numbers referred to batch numbers in the production process. A26E-311 is the Lotus part number, as referred to in the parts manual

Sanville had to try to sort out the problem—the delays were costly while Lotus waited for usable heads. Eventually, John Standen persuaded William Mills to sand-cast the heads, which they did, and all the head problems were solved immediately, including the head-gasket failures which, with hindsight, were realized to be caused by a combination of two things. Firstly, the original heads from Birmid were not stiff enough

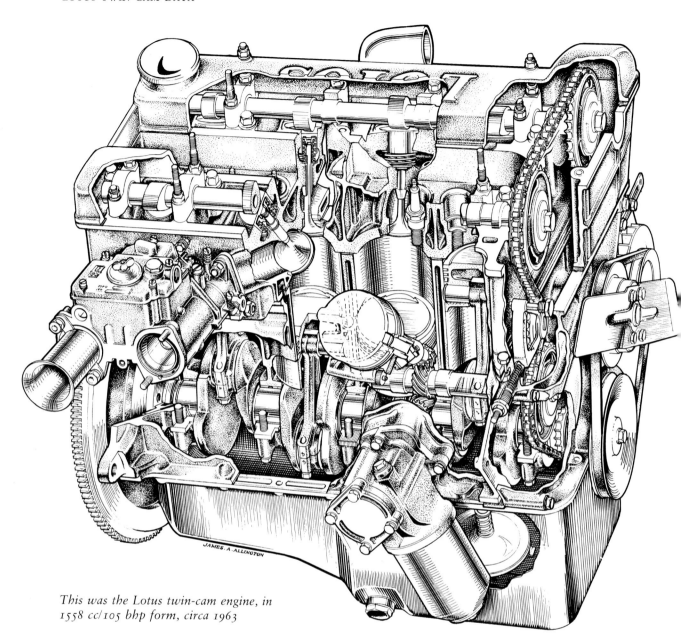

*This was the Lotus twin-cam engine, in
1558 cc/105 bhp form, circa 1963*

and moved around under load and expansion.
Secondly, the original gasket material was not up
to the job. The only other later modifications
made to the head were to add a bridge piece
between numbers 2 and 3 plugs, and a stiffening
web to the inlet tract. William Mills sand-cast
them to the end. No records exist of how many
die-cast heads were made.

Another problem was that of the con-rods.
Keith Duckworth had long maintained that the
standard items were not strong enough and had
already produced his own rods for his Cortina
engines (see Chapter 6). The original rods were

standard Ford items specially selected for Lotus—
hence the L-type name. These could cope with the
normal Cortina power, but not with the increased
output of the twin-cam. In fact, if the L-type could
be classified as the A-type Lotus rod, there was a
B-type designed by Joe Rolando who, unfortunately, detailed too sharp a radius on the eye
section, and before anything could be done, Ford
had already made around 2000 useless rods! The
design was then modified to give the 125E C-type
rod, with its stronger section and larger bolt,
which is still being produced today. These went
into all engines built from December 1963.

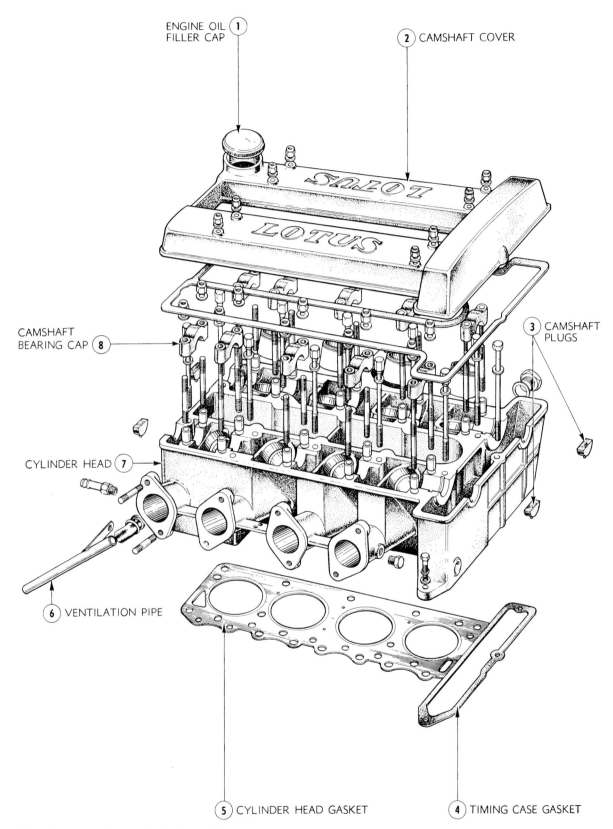

ENGINE OIL (1)
FILLER CAP

(2) CAMSHAFT COVER

CAMSHAFT
BEARING CAP (8)

(3) CAMSHAFT
PLUGS

CYLINDER HEAD (7)

(6) VENTILATION PIPE

(5) CYLINDER HEAD GASKET

(4) TIMING CASE GASKET

A Ford-produced 'exploded' view of the
cylinder-head assembly

Twin Cam Block

Minimum cylinder wall thickness = 0.100 in. Stamp block grade 'LB' on front face of block. This block to be used for the 1558 cc engine *only*. It is unsuitable for reboring to 83.5 mm (1600 cc) or 85 mm (1650 cc).

Minimum cylinder wall thickness = 0.140 in. Stamp block grade 'LA' on front face of block. This block can be used for the 1558 cc engine, or rebored to 83.5 mm for 1600 cc engines, or rebored to 85.0 mm for 1650 cc engines.

Minimum cylinder wall thickness = 0.140 in. Standard 82.55 mm bore, outside specification for size, finish, taper or ovality. Stamp block grade 'LAA' on front face of block. This block is *unsuitable for use on 1558 cc engines*, but may be rebored to 83.5 mm for 1600 cc engines, or to 85.0 mm for 1650 cc engines.

Block grade 'LAA' enables blocks which would otherwise be scrap to be used on high performance engines.

Ford graded all the blocks for use at Lotus, as they did the crankshafts, which were stiffer and balanced to a higher tolerance than normal. Pistons were graded, and special main and big-end bearings were used.

Steve Sanville was now production engineer and had complete responsibility for having the engines built. One other problem he faced was not being able to remove casting sand trapped around the number four exhaust areas, which resulted in high wear between the cam follower and head due to gritty oil laying around unable to drain. On the inlet side, oil drained away down the pushrod holes. Eventually, steel sleeves were put in on the exhaust side but, in the end, it was easier to let JAP sleeve all inlet and exhaust valve guides,

Left
This sums up the suitability, or otherwise, of various Ford cylinder blocks for use in Lotus twin-cam engines

Below
Block identification can be found on the top left-hand corner. This one is 'LA'

From late 1964 the Lotus-Cortina Mk I received a facelift. Note the 'Cortina' name on the bonnet, and the wider grille surrounding the turn/indicator lights

which was done by mid-1964. Actually, Steve made a cross-drilling modification across number four exhaust in 1966 that allowed any sand to be removed. After this, there was really no need to sleeve at all, but this practice continued until the end.

Fortunately for Fred Bushell, the dealers and Ford, the Elan and the Lotus-Cortina began to be produced in sufficient quantities from June 1963 to retrieve the sticky situation, and in 1964 Cheshunt produced 1762 cars, 567 of which were Lotus-Cortinas. Also in November 1964 the Series 2 Elan was announced, and after the S/E version was introduced, it was Steve and his team who changed the jets and chokes in the Webers, put in the S/E camshafts and repainted the cam cover at Cheshunt after the standard engine had already been assembled by JAP.

At last a pattern had been established on the road-going cars until the liquidation of JAP, which was mainly forced upon them by very restrictive union practices (something which was totally alien to the Lotus workforce). Villiers of Wolverhampton bought out JAP, took over some of their tooling, and then machined and assembled the engine. However, instead of being built at Tottenham, it was now made at Wolverhampton, and the distances involved were to play a large part in the job, the blocks being sent from Dagenham to Wolverhampton, and completed engines being sent back down to Cheshunt.

Villiers then became Norton Villiers after they took over the Norton, Matchless, AJS motorcycle group. Norton Villiers also had very strong unions; Roy Badcock (who joined Lotus in 1955 and was service manager from 1970 to 1983) remembers, 'You couldn't even talk to the fitter on the line, everything was done through his foreman, and if on a bad day he didn't want to talk to you, that was it—very annoying after travelling from Cheshunt!'

The situation came to a head in 1966 when Colin Chapman found Hethel; the move from Cheshunt in November of that year also coincided with Ford's desire to assemble their own Lotus-Cortina (the Mk II). In fact, at this time, Lotus were unable to meet the demand for the engine, from both Ford and their own Elan project through Norton Villiers. Union disputes in the latter's workshop were causing delays in engine production. So the decision was taken to machine the heads themselves at Hethel. Roy was given six weeks to set up the machine shop at Hethel, and he achieved this in the allotted time. The head production rate increased three-fold—they were machined, guides and seats fitted, and studded, and were then returned to Norton Villiers for them to fit the valves and assemble to the rest of the engine.

Eventually, everything nearly ground to a halt as Norton Villiers floundered deeper and deeper into trouble with union disputes (ultimately, this was the reason for their demise, like JAP), and with heads being thrown at them they just gave up, even being unable to cope with assembly. Also, the transport logistics were unbelievably costly, for blocks were sent from Dagenham to Wolverhampton, head castings from Wednesbury to Hethel, machined heads from Hethel to Wolverhampton, assembled engines from Wolverhampton to Hethel and, when the Mk II Lotus-Cortina came along, engines from Hethel to Dagenham! So, in mid-1967, they decided to move everything to Hethel for Lotus to produce the engine themselves. Again, Roy had the task of setting it up; such was the fear of the unions at Norton Villiers that a cloak-and-dagger operation was mounted to retrieve the machines after working hours, for fear of being attacked. Fortunately, the move passed without incident, and once the equipment was installed at Hethel, the production of engines entered its final phase and the rate increased in leaps and bounds.

Steve Sanville and Colin Gane enjoyed a few epic journeys in early Lotus-Cortinas. One such occurred in 1963; they were in a Cortina registered 594 PJH going to Weber in Italy again, but with a spare engine projecting into the car from the boot—the rear seat had been removed—and the Italian customs man thought it was a new *bimotore* model, such as Alfa Romeo had built in the 1930s. After convincing him it was not, they continued. On the way back, first gear seized up while they were motoring along in top gear. The first gear started to revolve but was starved of oil due to a lubrication problem, causing it to seize on the main shaft. There was slight drama in stopping the car, but they limped to a hotel in third gear, took the gearbox out and flew home. All gearboxes were recalled by Ford because of this, and all were modified. Eventually, the

gearbox was taken to Italy in the Formula One transporter when the Lotus team went to Monza, and the car driven home.

Another time, the same two were on their way to Venice, dicing with an Alfa which was following them, when the sump plug fell out. The Alfa was not seen again, and a piece of wood acted as the new plug. On several occasions Steve and Colin experienced a fan blade coming off and modifying the bonnet; once it actually sliced through the bonnet and disappeared!

Other interesting work carried out at Cheshunt included a one-off redesign of the Elite rear suspension based on a Jaguar rubber system (this was done by Brian Luff in 1962)—apparently it felt like driving jelly and was not a success. Victor Grimwood, who stayed with Lotus, carried out a 'private' 1558 cc conversion to his Elite in 1963, and Roy McGregor remembers that a standard 1200 cc Cortina engine and gearbox were fitted in an Elan at the time, together with experimental

In 1965 the West Sussex police took delivery of 12 Lotus-Cortinas. Until these cars began to give trouble from the A-frame rear suspension, they were looked upon as the ultimate Q-cars. Nevertheless, they are remembered with great fondness by the Chichester police

solid drive shafts; he never knew why, as 'decisions were taken behind closed doors'. Also before the move to Hethel in 1966, Ford sent a Corsair to Cheshunt and a twin-cam engine was fitted. This was intended for production, but never actually saw the light of day. Immediately prior to the move to Hethel, Cheshunt built its one and only Mk II Lotus-Cortina for evaluation before its announcement; from then on, all Mk IIs were built by Ford at Dagenham, utilizing their standard Mk II Cortina bodies. The Mk II became far more rationalized with the standard car than the Mk I had ever been.

Mike Warner admits that 50 twin-cam engines were 'lost' by Lotus Components in the move from Cheshunt to Hethel; doubtless, someone did well, as they were never found.

3 Production at Hethel

The twin-cam engine enjoyed a trouble-free run from 1967 to the end in 1975. With better machining and better standardization than before, and incredible reliability, the Hethel-built engines were supreme in terms of build quality. Lotus was free of all the union disputes, there were no transport problems, and engineers were able to keep an eye on things at all times. The move to Hethel also coincided with Ford's update of the engine for the Mk II versions of the Cortina, and the blocks were now specially cast for Lotus, having a large 'L' cast into the right-hand engine-mounting area. The crankshafts were graded more carefully than before, and carried six instead of four flywheel bolts. A new rear oil seal was made, together with new oil pick-up pipes and

strainer, a different sump and a two-piece back-plate instead of the old one-piece plate. The main-bearing caps were stronger and square in section, rather than the original round-shouldered type. A higher grade of piston was also used (C-type instead of the old A-type). These changes were made in August 1967 after approximately 7100 1558 cc engines had been assembled by JAP and Norton Villiers in a four-year period (compare this to the final total number of 32,600 in 1975, i.e. Hethel made 25,500 engines in only eight years).

For Roy Badcock and Steve Sanville, the first task at Hethel was to install a washing/degreasing

Below left
Ford publicity shot of the Lotus-Cortina Mk II, still in white with green stripes

Below
The engine bay of the 1967 Lotus-Cortina Mk II. Note the revised air-filter arrangement. From 1968 on, the cam cover would be black with the name 'Lotus' across the front of the casting

plant for the blocks and to make up test-beds for the engine. The head machining area, together now with front-cover and backplate machining positions, had already been set up. The assembly line at Hethel employed between 16 and 20 men, most of whom were ex-RAF fitters, hired because of their high standard of work. Indeed, the overall quality of build evolved to an extremely high standard. On the line each man had a specific task to do, and did not build up his own engine in the Aston Martin manner.

The test procedure at Hethel never varied from 1967 to the end—all engines were hot run for one hour not exceeding 3000 rpm, and one in every 50 was fully run in and then power tested less ancillaries. This was one of the reasons, together with even better sand-casting of the head by William Mills, better machining and better build, why there were negligible warranty claims (see later). Throughout the engine's life, apart from the production changes introduced, it stayed the same.

Above
A Halewood-built Escort Twin Cam production car, complete with the facelift circular headlamps. Note the 'Twin Cam' badges on the flanks

Below
The Twin Cam badge on the Escort, as also fitted to Lotus Seven S3 models with twin-cam engines

With engines for Ford firstly going to Dagenham for use in the Mk II Lotus-Cortina in 1967, then from 1968 to Halewood near Liverpool for the new Escort Twin Cam, the production rate was about 100 engines a week—also the Lotus +2 had started to come on stream in 1967. This figure was boosted to a regular maximum of 120 engines a week into 1971 and then it fell away to 80–85 a week until the end. All engine deliveries for Ford stopped in 1971 with the demise of the Escort Twin Cam, but the Elan Sprint, +2S130 and the Europa (which had gained a twin-cam) were all selling well. Production never officially ceased, but simply faded away in 1975, after a staggering build rate of four to six engines a week per man throughout the Hethel production period. The twin-cam engine remains one of the all-time greats in terms of performance, output for its size, and also in terms of race and rally victories—a classic.

4 Pre-Big Valve and Stromberg engines

Two things happened in 1968 that were to change the course of the engine's career. Firstly, Steve Sanville and his team began building extra-powerful twin-cam engines based on a new camshaft, to be known as the Super Special Equipment cam (D-type). This was drawn up by Ron Burr and detailed in application by Graham Atkin. It was based on the high-lift, five-bearing Coventry Climax FWA 3060 camshaft, as used in the Stage III FWE engines (for Elites) giving 105 bhp. These SSE engines also had 0.040 in. shaved off the head, increasing the compression ratio to 10.3:1, and slight ignition advance, bigger chokes in the Weber carburettors together with different jets, and were giving 124–125 bhp. The engine predates the Big Valve unit by a full two years and was performing on the original, standard-size valves. So why didn't the SSE engine find its way into the Elans and +2s? Well, in truth, a few did, being known as the Super Weber S/E. No doubt, Graham Arnold, who was Lotus' sales manager at the time, had some put into his notoriously fast press cars. Indeed, the late John Bolster, of *Autosport*, wondered why his 1971 production Sprint never went as fast as the press +2 car (NAH 120F with a 3.9 diff.) which weighed considerably more.

The sole reason for this engine not being put into cars was the limitation set by the soft rubber Rotoflex drive-shaft couplings, which allowed too much wind-up and surge when the extra power and torque were put through them. One day, after he saw Steve in a +2 going around the test track, Colin Chapman remarked, 'God, was that you lurching around out there?' Steve was using an Elan S3 as his development hack with one of his Super S/E engines installed. This really was the predecessor of the future Sprint.

The second occurrence had a more far-reaching effect. After the Earls Court Motor Show in October 1968, where the S4 Elan was announced, Dennis Austin, the company's buyer, realized that Zenith-Stromberg carburettors cost far less than Webers. As Lotus was going through yet another financial crisis at the time, Steve Sanville received a letter summoning him to report to Colin Chapman, when he was promptly told to put Strombergs on the engine.

In spite of having to alter the head casting to suit the new carburettors, and carrying out all the testing, the whole operation still cost less than using Webers. It was Graham Atkin's responsibility to redesign the head and to do all the detailed work. He joined Lotus on 1 April 1967 and worked with Steve on the production side and on the Super S/Es. He left Lotus, with Steve, in October 1969 to found Norvic Racing Engines in Wymondham, returned to Hethel at the end of 1970, left again in October 1979 to go to Jaguar Rover Triumph, then returned to Lotus in August 1985. The head was to retain the same internal pieces as the Weber head, as the internal core could not be changed—the brief was to avoid unnecessary expense. New core equipment was made for the siamezed inlet ports and was cast into the head. The original core for the Weber head was done in this way—the head and port cores are, in effect, two separate castings. In fact, the original prototype ports were bolted on to the head.

Graham carried out many experiments to get a reasonable flow into the combustion chambers—if the ports themselves were biased in any one direction (as opposed to a true siamezed layout), the flow was horrendous. Also if the razor edge dividing the ports was moved 1 mm either way,

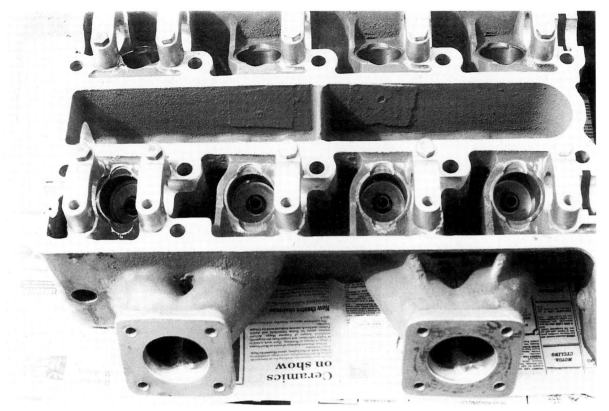

the flow was disrupted. Eventually, either by chance or by scientific judgement, Graham found that by blunting off the razor edge at the fork, the air flow became perfectly balanced on a true siamezed port.

The inlet tracts of the Stromberg head are longer than those of the Weber version, but the overall length with the carburettors and air box fitted is the same. Solex, who produced the Stromberg carburettors, did all the work on the temperature compensators, needles and settings for the 175 CDS Stromberg, and all the testing was done by ERA (which was part of the Solex Group) at Dunstable.

It is important to note that domestic-market cars had Strombergs before those destined for the USA because of the delay in preparing the emission engine. Graham also did all the emission work necessary for the engine to pass the Californian Air Resources Board (ARB) restraints—this was only for California, not the rest of the USA.

The aim was to achieve low hydro-carbon (HC) levels at start-up and slow speeds, and for this a means of warming the air/fuel mixture had to be devised. ERA, who did the testing, were the only people to have experience in this field, and the original engine (known as the Duplex engine in their report) had different Stromberg carburettors (175CDSE) developed by Solex for this application. Graham Atkin drew all the cross-pipe layout and the primary and secondary throttle arrangements so that the incoming cold air would mix with the fuel, cross to the exhaust side, where it was warmed, and then return to the inlet port. Retarding the ignition was found to help a quicker warm-up as well.

Strombergs had to be used in the emission application since Webers would not pass the test,

and they continued to be used in the Jensen Healey and Elite on the 2 litre Type 907 engines. The new tri-jet Dellortos easily cope with the emission regulations from 1986, and now there is no need to use Strombergs any more.

For the emission engines the test procedure was rigorous, there being a zero-mileage test, a 50,000-mile test and a final test. At the time, +2s were being driven around the Hethel test track, day and night, by teams of drivers to make up the 50,000 miles, and at every 4000 miles these cars went down to ERA for testing. If the engine passed the final test, it was signed off. This had to be done for each model year. The teams of drivers were recruited from factory personnel and local people. Colin Gane remembers being called out one Sunday morning after a local lad had gone to sleep at the wheel and had turned over a +2, which was upside down on its roof. The car was righted and placed in the workshop, and on Monday morning everyone saw the smashed +2 with the Stars and Stripes draped over it and a large notice saying 'passed'! In theory, no Elans were sold in the USA after 1968 because they would not pass the body side-intrusion crash test, whereas the +2 and later Europa would pass (the +2 because of its metal sill member and the Europa because of a deeper sill box-section and its seat-belt anchor plate).

Whether the cost of using the Strombergs was less in the end is not clear. Certainly, unless the carburettors were obtained free to offset all the testing procedures, design work and different mouldings for the Elan and +2 bonnet (which

Above left
A new, bare Stromberg head, having just been line-bored, and with bolts holding down the caps prior to having their respective numbers stamped on for identification. Siamezed ports can be seen clearly. All Stromberg heads were sand-cast by William Mills

Left
A Stromberg head showing the blunted-off junction in the siamezed ports

Right
The changing shape of the port divider

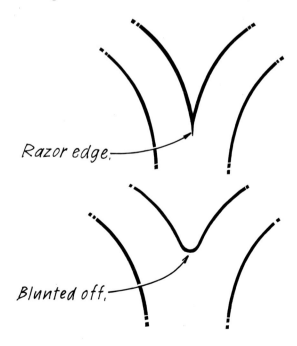

Razor edge.

Blunted off.

needed a bulge to clear the carburettor), it is difficult to believe that it was all justified for less than 18 months' domestic production—April 1969 until September 1970. The emission engines continued, of course, and all the Solex testing helped later on with the 2 litre 907 engines, so perhaps overall it was cheaper. However, a campaign was already under way within Lotus, led mainly by the sales people and the buyers, to reinstate the Webers, as without them the twin-cam engine was thought to look cissy. Webers had the macho image that everybody expected when the bonnet was lifted.

In spite of the Strombergs being disliked, Roy Badcock (then the service manager) preferred them because they gave better fuel economy and made the engines smoother over the entire rev range. They also produced some of the fastest Elans known, which were even quicker than a Sprint. All in all, they were better to drive behind than were the Webers. Even today many people at Hethel still prefer Strombergs, but fashion dictated the return of four trumpets.

There were only two problems with the Strombergs on the domestic market. The first, very minor, is that on idle the exhaust beat becomes very 'splashy' as it hunts, not a regular beat as with Webers or Dellortos. The second, which caused, and still causes, much heartache was icing up. At just above freezing point, at an ambient air temperature of 2–3 degrees Celsius, the in-rush of air, carrying with it moisture droplets, experiences a 10 degree Celsius drop

between entry and the venturi. The water vapour freezes around the needle, forms a solid obstruction and prevents it from rising and falling. Eventually, the carburettor butterflies ice up, causing the throttle to stick open; finally, no fuel gets through and the engine stops. The only cure for this is to wait for the ice to melt. On dry days icing does not occur, even down to −20 degrees Celsius; it only occurs on damp days at around 2–3 degrees Celsius.

To overcome the icing problem, Lotus experimented with the diversion of hot air from the exhaust manifold side into the air cleaner, but this did not help. It is simply something that one has to live with; history has repeated itself, too, for Excel S/Es experience icing with their new Dellortos, a problem finally solved in 1987.

Note that Stromberg-equipped engines also run 5 degrees Celsius hotter than Weber engines; up to 95 degrees Celsius is normal because of their leaner mixture and different port shape, and because with the introduction of the Strombergs, the full-width Coventry Radiator block was dropped in favour of the smaller type with ducting. This was unfortunate since the engine requires adequate cooling, which the early radiators always gave. With the new type, it is imperative that all the ducting is in place and that there are no obstructions in front of the radiator. Consequently, overheating is more prevalent with Stromberg engines than it is with those using Webers or Dellortos.

5 The Big Valve engine— con or sales gimmick?

At the 1968 London Motor Show Colin Chapman offered Tony Rudd the job of replacing Ron Hickman (of Elite, Elan and +2 evolvement, and later the designer of the famous Black & Decker Workmate bench), but he did not agree to join Lotus until after the Dutch GP at Zandvoort in June 1969. In effect, he took over from Steve Sanville, who had also decided to leave (together with Graham Atkin).

Tony's first job was to supervise the final stages of the 2 litre Type 907 engine development; Ron Burr had reached the final drawing stage and Tony had to simplify the engine for production. In June 1970 he was appointed engineering director, and promptly had to make a large number of engineering staff redundant because of falling sales. He was also involved in longer-term projects, namely the M50 Elite (Type 75), M52 Eclat (Type 76) and M70 Esprit (Type 79). Also projected, even though the 907 engine had not been built yet, were the M51, M53 and M71 V8 versions, which were to have what would be, in effect, two 907 engines stuck together. It is interesting to note that the Europa replacement was already being considered in 1970, too, six years before it finally came on to the scene. Finally, one more project which never came to fruition was the M60, a stretched +2S with a Type 907 engine in it—a pity.

Tony already had his hands reasonably full when, in early October 1970, Colin Chapman came into his office, and the Big Valve engine was born out of their conversation, which went like this:

Tony Rudd, engineering director of Lotus for many years

'Things are a bit iddely-umpty! Got to improve the image of the Elan and +2. You're the engineering director, what can you do?' asked Colin.

'How about an honest increase in power, not the "go-faster" stripes?' Tony replied. (At the time Graham Arnold, the sales director, wanted to introduce a Gold Leaf Elan to pep up the image.)

Colin said, 'How long will it take and how much?'

'About a week.'

'If it's only going to take a week, it can't cost very much, so get on with it!'

Tony reckoned on getting at least a 20 per cent increase on the standard 105 bhp engine, i.e. 125–130 bhp. When eventually the press reported on the new version, confusion arose because 126 bhp is not a 20 per cent increase over the 118 bhp

of the S/E Stromberg unit. All Rudd had had to do was amend the BRM work which had been done years earlier to make it suitable for production. The compression ratio was increased by skimming 0.040 in. off the head, the port shapes were improved and there were bigger inlet valves, different chokes and jets in the Webers and a modified camshaft to give a smoother, better torque curve.

But what should we believe? After all, Steve Sanville and Graham Atkin had produced Big Valve power (124–125 bhp), without the big valve, two years earlier, the camshaft already existed in that engine and the domestic Stromberg-carbureted units from 1969 onwards, while Keith Duckworth could easily achieve 140–145 bhp on standard-size valves. The big inlet valve is only 0.036 in. larger than the normal valve

and was conceived mathematically. As Steve Sanville pointed out, a new form tool was produced to open out the ports to suit the valve which, therefore, gave better production tolerances than the original cast port. He maintains that the big valve was put in as a gimmick. Whatever the reason, the total gain from it was no more than 1 bhp.

After ten days, Colin phoned Tony to ask, 'Where's the b—— head?', when in fact it was already being fitted into an Elan, so Colin ordered the car to be left in his parking bay so that he could take it home. Everybody prayed until lunch time the next day when Tony's phone rang again: 'Do you go out for lunch?' 'Yes.' 'Well, take the car, and use all the power in all of the gears at all times.' Tony did and was surprised. That same afternoon Colin gave the go-ahead.

The four twin-cam engined Lotus passenger cars in a group, all sharing the Big Valve engine. The Seven has a Holbay unit; the Europa is a 1973 Special; the Sprint is a factory-converted S4 (hence the bulged Stromberg bonnet and the silver wheels); and the +2 is a 1973 +2S130

The only modifications needed to cope with the increased power and torque were to fit a brace across the differential mounting lugs and to install the interleaved Rotoflex couplings, which were considerably stiffer than the original types. An argument then ensued over what to call the new engine—'Big Valve' or '130 bhp'. In the end, there was a compromise with Graham Arnold, who got his Sprint with Gold Leaf colours and stripes plus a Big Valve engine, while the +2 became the +2S130. The engine was announced at the 1970

London Motor Show in a very distinctive Elan which was painted satin matt black over yellow.

So the Big Valve work was done in precisely ten days, and even if it was a gimmick, it certainly worked, as sales revived after all the new Big Valve marketing had been completed. Maybe it was just a ploy to raise sales, but it was incredibly cheap to do during yet another Lotus cash crisis. Tony Rudd certainly takes the credit, as he was there at the time, whereas Steve Sanville and Graham Atkin had left. He made it suitable for production and he already knew how to make twin-cams go from his days at Bourne. On the other hand, Steve and Graham produced their Super S/E Weber engines in exactly the same form (less the big inlet valve) two years earlier when Tony was not yet at Hethel, and these gave all but the same power. In fact, Steve's Weber choke and jet settings were identical to those of the Big Valve. At that time, the limitations were with the Rotoflex couplings.

The Stromberg S/E gave 118 bhp and went incredibly quickly (0–100 mph in 20.0 seconds—*Motor* road test, April 1970). The Sprint only had an extra 8 bhp and 5 lb ft torque, but required a differential brace and stronger couplings, yet in the *Motor* test of March 1971 it was slower (0–100 mph in 20.3 seconds) than the Stromberg S/E. Academic maybe, but possibly the package was designed to allow the price to go up, yet had to give something in return—an impression of more power and speed over previous Elans and +2s.

Generally, the Big Valve unit is not as smooth as the Weber S/E version, and the cam delivers maximum torque at 5500 rpm instead of at the 4000 rpm of the Weber S/E. To combat this, acceleration was enhanced by fitting a 3.77:1 final-drive ratio as standard, as opposed to the 3.55:1 ratio of the S/E. A Big Valve with the optional 3.55:1 diff gave slower acceleration times but was the fastest of all on top speed. (Don McLaughlin, the Lotus PR chief, recalls doing 134 mph in Belgium in a Sprint, which dropped to 128 mph with the headlamps up!)

Taken overall, the Sprint package certainly revived sales, the emphasis being on more power (the Weber macho image had returned, at last), but with it came the inevitable price increases. However, the sight of a new black-crackle Big Valve cam cover, together with a stripey Gold Leaf paint scheme, worked wonders—but surely it was a sales gimmick?

Big Valve engine production finally came to an

Pure elegance—the ultimate in twin-cam-era cars. It is, of course, the Lotus Elan +2S130. This particular example is a 1973 model with a four-speed gearbox

end, without ceremony, in 1975.

While talking to Tony Rudd, I gleaned some other interesting facts. In 1971 he was developing a five-speed gearbox for use in the new Elite model, and he realized that by changing the selector mechanism this could also be fitted to the +2. The result was that the five-speed +2s were initially no more than test-beds for the Elite. The Big Valve engine could just cope with the low ratios of the gearbox (a five-speed +2S130 is slower off the mark than a four-speed model), and

clearly there was no torque-capacity problem as the new gearbox was designed to cope with the 160 bhp of the new 2 litre Type 907 engine.

Tony also told me that valve stem seals were never fitted to the twin-cam (to stop oil running down the guides), quite simply because production tolerances would not allow it. However, for rebuilt engines to be properly assembled, the guides should be pipe reamed; this gives circular machine marks, and with correct Lotus-specification valves no wear should occur. Unfortunately, the guides have to be reamed in situ; if the valve stems are rough these will trap grit, eventually marking the guide and causing wear. This produces the well-known Lotus oil haze from the exhaust. Correct machining of the guides is critically important.

6 Race and rally engines

The twin-cam engine was, and still is, unsurpassed in terms of race-winning performances in both international and national events. The only other engine to enjoy such a run was the Coventry Climax FPF twin-cam in all its guises (from 1.5 to 2.7 litres), but that was not a production road-car engine built in such large numbers as the Lotus twin-cam. The Alfa Romeo twin-cam engines, in 1300, 1600, 1750 and 2000 cc forms, are also supremely successful as production road engines but not in terms of race victories. Surprisingly, the Lotus engine was usually employed in road cars used for competition, namely the Elan 26R, Lotus 47 and the Ford Lotus-Cortina and Escort Twin Cam. The exceptions were the Lotus 23B sports racer and a few of the Lotus 35 Formula 2 and Formula 3 cars entrusted to Ron Harris to run on behalf of Lotus.

The twin-cam race engine is completely different from the road engine, but having said that, engine preparers were limited in how far they could go to achieve the maximum power. Only so many different racing components can go into the basic cylinder block and head, and each specialist had his own tweak to do. It is ironic that after its racing demise, people today still base everything on Cosworth or BRM preparations and cam profiles. Many famous names lent their expertise during its racing history, but at the start it was Keith Duckworth, who engineered the first Lotus-Cortina racing engines for Group 2 competition. He realized the need for beefier conrods, different pistons and a crankshaft with more counterbalance weights on it. He also proceeded to rework the head (as we have seen already), but retained standard valves. He built up a stronger bottom end, using his own rods, pistons and steel main caps in place of the cast-iron standard items.

In this form, 140–145 bhp on Weber 40 DCOEs was obtained, and in 1964 a customer's racing version was offered giving 140 bhp.

Cosworth produced these engines for Colin, until one day he sat next to Tony Rudd of BRM at a lunch given by Champion at the Savoy Hotel in London after the 1964 Lord Mayor's Show. Colin asked Tony about the possibility of working on the twin-cam engine, and the deal was finalized in the toilet! The reasoning is unclear. Why the change? Perhaps, at the time, Cosworth were overloaded with work, perhaps Colin thought BRM would be better—who knows? In any case, Cosworth continued to build and supply Lotus race engines. BRM were ultimately responsible for all the Elan 26R engines and the Lotus-Cortina and 47 race engines. For the 26Rs, the blocks and the heads were sent from Cheshunt to Bourne. BRM fitted their own crankshaft, con-rods and pistons, gas-flowed and ported the head, fitted bigger valves and their own camshafts. The engines were usually enlarged to 1594 cc and gave around 160–165 bhp on Weber carburettors. The fully-built engines were returned to Cheshunt where they were mated to the appropriate body/chassis unit under the Lotus Components banner.

During the development period BRM experienced head-gasket failures at high rpm, as had happened in the original concept programme, and a few special stronger heads were sand-cast by Aeroplane and Motor. These helped, together with the use of different head-gasket material. Eventually, the William Mills sand-cast head was used, as it was already in production, and the current standard Coopers head gasket retained.

BRM offered four states of tune: Phase I gave 130–140 bhp; Phase II gave 140+ bhp; Phase III

VEGANTUNE 69

The Vegantune 1969 range of engines will incorporate small modifications to ease Owner/Driver maintenance.

Steel tappets used with Hydural bronze valve guides, inlet and exhaust valve specification improved to give 100% safe valve gear. All camshafts heat treated and manufactured from fresh blanks to eliminate the possibility of breakage. Con-rods remain the same as on previous engines. (Over 1,000 rods of this type in use without a single breakage). The crankshaft has been modified to obtain better counter balance. All engines incorporate the Mk. 3 oil pump removing all possibility of oil leakage from this component.

The quoted power output remains at our conservative 170 B.H.P. minimum for the 1600 c.c. unit, the torque curve is improved on all types. An exchange component system is to be introduced for all engines. In addition to the 1600 c.c. and 1300 c.c. engines an 1100 c.c. unit is introduced for Formula 'C'.

69 FLB

Capacity 1600 c.c.
Bore   83.5 mm.
Stroke   72.5 mm.
Output   170 B.H.P. min.

An all steel unit with a power curve unsurpassed for F.B. racing.

69 FLC

Capacity 1600 c.c.
Bore   83.5 m.m.
Stroke   72.5 m.m.
Output   185 B.H.P. min.

Similar to the FLB but fitted with Lucas petrol injection giving more power and torque throughout the range.

69 FLE

Capacity 1300 c.c.
Bore   83.5 mm.
Stroke   59.3 mm.
Output   150 B.H.P. min.

Similar to the FLB, available with P.I. or carburettors

69 FLG

Capacity 1100 c.c.
Bore   83.5 mm.
Stroke   50.2 mm.
Output   140 B.H.P. min.

This engine revs very freely and has excellent torque curve. Available with P.I. or carburettors.

NOTE: Engine Nos. designated /2 are fitted with built-in alternator and tooth belt drive. This extra available on all engines.

Above
From the Vegantune brochure of 1969, this shows the various types of competition twin-cam engine which were available

Left
Steel bearing caps gave added strength to the bottom end of a race-tuned twin-cam by Vegantune

Above
Racing versions of the Elan were known as Type 26R. This car is pictured at the 1964 Brands Hatch British GP

Overleaf
BRM boosted the performance of twin-cam engines to help produce really sparkling Elans. This is what Patrick McNally thought of a BRM-Elan in 1967. Courtesy Autosport

Road Test by
PATRICK McNALLY

THE LOTUS ELAN BRM

FOLLOWING the current trend of famous racing names joining forces to produce a single car comes the Lotus Elan BRM, the brain-child of works BRM driver Mike Spence, whose concern in Maidenhead is marketing this machine.

The Lotus Elan is already a highly successful 2-seater sports car with superlative roadholding, a first-class gearbox coupled with a reasonably luxurious interior and powerful brakes. The BRM version is basically the same, with the exception of its high performance engine, specially developed by the BRM development division of Rubery Owen, which gives the car a maximum speed of 130 mph and a 0-60 time comparable to an E-type Jaguar or a DB6 Vantage Aston Martin. The Lotus BRM is finished in the BRM colours of polychromatic dark green with blaze orange bumpers, which certainly make it distinctive enough.

There are many different ways of extracting more power from the ubiquitous Ford twin-cam engine, but most of them either make the engine inflexible or unreliable, and in some cases do both. BRM's development programme on racing versions of this unit over the last couple of seasons has given them such information as to make it possible for them to produce a 130 bhp engine which is just as reliable and flexible as the standard motor. Every engine is completely dismantled at the BRM works in Bourne, and the following modifications are made: the cylinder head has 0.010 ins removed from its face and the inlet and exhaust ports are extensively modified to increase the air-flow. The inlet valves are replaced by BRM units with 1.55 ins diameter heads, the standard exhaust valves being retained. The cylinder block has 0.020 ins machined from its top face to give 0.014 ins squish deck height to the piston—trueing the cylinder block also ensures a perfect seal between the block and head. The crankshaft is dynamically balanced and the flywheel and clutch assembly are assured of constant union by being double dowelled. As the latest versions of the Ford twin-cam engine are fitted with

C-type rods which are good for 7000 rpm, these are retained but are balanced along with the pistons to very fine limits. To ensure good lubrication the oil pressure relief valve spring is changed for a stronger one which gives an oil pressure of 55-65 psi at running speeds. There are two different types of camshaft available, the CPL 2 and the L1; the former gives 130 bhp, and the latter 140 bhp. The standard 40 DCOE Weber carburetters are retained, but 33 mm chokes and 130 main jets and 170 air correction jets are fitted. The exhaust system, which is one of the weakest points of a standard Elan,

as it restricts the engine breathing considerably, is changed for a fabricated four-branch manifold with a large diameter pipe and a "special equipment" silencer—a straight-through muffler can be specified at no extra cost. Before every engine leaves the factory after being meticulously assembled, it is bench-tested to ensure it produces the correct number of horses. If the engine's power curve falls short by more than 2.5 bhp it is not released.

When I was asked to road-test the car prior to its announcement I was far from convinced that the character of the Elan would be changed in any major way. But the effect of 130 bhp changes the whole nature of the car. The fully independent suspension of the Lotus Elan can cope ably with the standard engine, but when the extra horsepower is added, so is a great deal of excitement. The roadholding is still first-

class, but much more fun can be experienced as the car can be driven far more on the throttle, and requires more skill and handling.

Starting the car from cold is no problem, but when the engine is hot, as with all Weber carburetted cars, it is better for the throttle to be depressed fully to provide a leaner mixture. Pumping the throttle will result in wet plugs. When the engine bursts into life it settles back to idle at 750 rpm without the least sign of lumpiness. The particular car I drove had no cut-out fitted to the distributor, and I was told I could use 7000 rpm in the gears and what I could get in top. The engine was as clean as a whistle all the way through the rev range, with not a flat spot anywhere—a remarkable achievement.

In far from ideal conditions with limited time the performance figures were taken, and to add to our troubles the engine was still relatively tight, having covered only 200 miles. Nevertheless the performance figures were little short of incredible: 0-60 mph was reached in 6.8 secs, with 80 mph coming up in 11.4 secs. The 0-100 figure started off at 18.2 secs, but towards the end of the test some better times were recorded. However in the interests of consistency all the acceleration figures quoted, with the exception of the quarter-mile, were taken during the initial part of the test and not towards the end, when the engine became noticeably more free. The real telltale is of course the quarter-mile which was covered in the mean time of 15.1 secs. Maximum speed recorded was 128.63 mph at 7000 rpm, but this was not a true indication of the absolute maximum of the car as a strong cross wind was having an adverse effect, and I have no hesitation at all in describing this as a true 130 mph car. In fact, in coupé form with a different axle ratio one could expect a speed well in excess of this. The speeds in the gears were 42 mph, 63 mph and 95 mph, for the car was fitted with the standard four-speed close-ratio Ford gearbox with ratios of 2.97, 2.01 and 1.40 to 1, with a final drive ratio of 3.55 to 1. An ultra-close-ratio gearbox is available.

Apart from the obvious performance advantages of the extra horsepower, the BRM-tuned power unit also encouraged the most enthusiastic cornering techniques, as there is sufficient power available to sort out any difficulties encountered. The test car had the optional straight-through silencer, but even so was not aggressively noisy, and there was certainly no increase of mechanical noise in the engine itself.

As the rest of the car, with the exception of the exterior finish, is standard we will not dwell too much on this subject. All Elans have first-class gearboxes, suspension systems and steering, and the increased horsepower was no problem for the servo four-wheel disc-brakes which stood up remarkably well to the test, though they did suffer a slight tendency to pull to the right towards the end of the test. Oil consumption would appear to be approximately a quart for 600 miles, but this figure may be slightly pessimistic as the engine was not fully run-in, and with piston rings well bedded-in it could be expected to drop to half this. Fuel consumption is about 25 mpg, but this depends very much on how the car is driven.

The BRM polychromatic green, much to my surprise, looks very attractive, especially when emphasized against the blaze orange bumpers. The whole effect is remarkably sophisticated for what might appear to the layman to be a rather jazzy scheme. The tasteful BRM insignia below the Lotus badge on the front of the car is the final touch, though it does rather give the game away. This fact was rather surprisingly drawn to my attention by a small boy in a Buckinghamshire village who turned to his mother and said with great aplomb "That, Mum, is a Lotus BRM."

The car is available both in coupé and hardtop form, either special equipment (£1,650) or standard (£1,525). Though the car tested was the 130 bhp version, the 140 bhp with the L1 camshafts is exactly the same price. Further details may be obtained from Mike Spence Ltd, Eland House, 11 High Street, Maidenhead, Berks, who are the sole distributors.

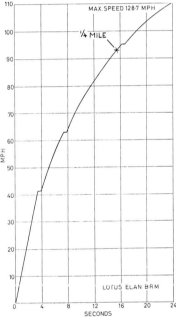

SPECIFICATION AND PERFORMANCE DATA

Car Tested: Lotus Elan BRM Special Equipment, price £1,650 in component form.

Engine: Four cylinders, 82.55 mm x 72.75 mm (1558 cc). Twin chain-driven overhead camshafts. Compression ratio 9·5 to 1. 130 bhp at 6500 rpm. Two twin choke Weber carburetters. Lucas coil and distributor.

Transmission: Single dry plate clutch. Four-speed all-synchromesh gearbox ratios 1, 1.40, 2.01, 2.97 to 1. Chassis-mounted Hypoid final drive unit, ratio 3.55 to 1.

Chassis: Steel central backbone chassis. Independent front suspension by wishbones and helical springs. Rack and pinion steering. Independent rear suspension by bottom wishbones and struts with helical springs. Telescopic dampers all round. Disc brakes front and rear with servo assistance. Centre-locking disc wheels with three-eared caps, fitted 145 x 13 SP41 tyres.

Equipment: 12-volt lighting and starting. Speedometer. Rev counter. Ammeter. Oil pressure, water temperature, and fuel gauges. Heating and demisting. Variable speed windscreen wipers and washers. Electrically controlled windows. Flashing direction indicators. Radio (extra).

Dimensions: Wheelbase 7 ft. Track 4 ft. Overall length 12 ft 1¼ ins. Width 4 ft 8 ins. Turning circle 29 ft 9 ins. Weight 13 cwt (dry).

Performance: Maximum speed 128.63 mph at 7000 rpm. Speeds in gears: 3rd, 95 mph; 2nd, 63 mph; 1st, 42 mph. Standing quarter-mile, 15.1 secs, terminal velocity, 93 mph. 0-30 mph, 2.65 secs. 0-50 mph, 5.2 secs. 0-60 mph, 6.8 secs. 0-80 mph, 11.4 secs. 0-100 mph, 18.1 secs.

Fuel Consumption: 25 mpg.

LOTUS ELAN B.R.M. & LOTUS ELAN S/E B.R.M.

SPECIFICATION

SPECIFICATION AS PER CURRENT LOTUS MODELS WITH THE FOLLOWING ALTERATIONS:-

ENGINE

Every engine is completely dismantled at the B.R.M. works in Bourne, Lincolnshire.

Cylinder head: Inlet and exhaust ports extensively modified to increase air flow and individually air flowed. .010" removed from fire face to improve compression ratio.

Cylinder Block: .020 in.removed from top face of block to give .014 in. squish deck height to piston.

Crankshaft, Flywheel & Clutch Assembly: Dynamically balanced and double dowelled.

Pistons and Connecting rods: fully balanced.

Inlet Valves: Replaced by B.R.M. valves with 1.550 in. dia. head.

Camshafts: Cosworth CPL2 camshafts are fitted as standard. For competition use only, L1 camshafts may be specified at no extra cost.

Lubrication system: fitted with high rate oil pressure relief valve spring to give oil pressure of 55 - 65 p.s.i. at running speeds.

Exhaust system: Fabricated four branch manifold with large diameter pipe and Elan S/E silencer. For competition use a Jaguar 'E' type straight through silencer can be specified at no extra cost.

Carburettor: 33 m.m. chokes are fitted and main and air correction jets are fitted to suit the engine on the test bed.

Every engine is meticulously assembled and bench tested for the following power out-puts (corrected): -

CPL2 Camshafts: 130 (plus or minus 2.5) B.H.P.

L1 Camshafts: 140 (plus or minus 2.5) B.H.P.

COACHWORK

Finished in B.R.M. Polychromatic Dark Green with Blaze Orange bumpers. The car sports both famous Lotus and B.R.M. badges.

For further details and road test car please contact Mr. Peter Davies at the sole distributors, Mike Spence Ltd., Eland House, 11 High Street, Maidenhead, Berks. Telephone: 28539.

Above left and left
Ultimate-tune BRM-prepared Lotus-Cortina twin-cam, enlarged to 1594 cc and using Lucas mechanical fuel injection. Note the 'BRM' engine plate and the different type of oil-filler cap. The injector unit was belt driven from the nose of the inlet camshaft

Above
Mike Spence Ltd issued a detailed specification of engine modifications for the BRM-prepared cars, for which they were renowned

PRICE LIST

LOTUS ELAN B.R.M.

PRICE IN COMPONENT FORM .... £1,560. 0. 0.

Optional Extras

Taurus thermostatically controlled oil radiator	21.	0.	0.
Knock-on wheels	29.	0.	0.
3.5 Diff ratio	23.	0.	0.
Close ratio gears	25.	0.	0.
Radio (Radiomobile) inc. suppressor kit .	40.	0.	0.
Radio suppressor kit only	4.	10.	0.
Inertia Reel Seat Belts	14.	0.	0.
Servo assisted brakes (with harder pads)	19.	0.	0.
Tonneau cover	12.	0.	0.
Firestone F100 Tyres	9.	0.	0.
Dunlop SP41 Tyres	9.	0.	0.
Workshop manual	4.	4.	0.
Triplex heated rear window	19.	0.	0.
Leather rim steering wheel	8.	0.	0.

B.R.M. Steel connecting rods: Price on application.

LOTUS ELAN SPECIAL EQUIPMENT B.R.M.

PRICE IN COMPONENT FORM .... £1,685. 0. 0.

Optional Extras

Taurus thermostatically controlled oil radiator	21.	0.	0.
Close ratio gears	25.	0.	0.
Radio (Radiomobile) inc. Suppressor kit	40.	0.	0.
Radio suppressor kit only	4.	10.	0.
Tonneau cover	12.	0.	0.
Workshop manual	4.	4.	0.
Triplex heated rear window	19.	0.	0.

B.R.M. Steel connecting rods: Price on application.

TERMS: Deposit required with order: £250. 0. 0d.
Balance payable on collection/delivery of car.

For further details and road test car please contact Mr. Peter Davies
at the sole distributors, Mike Spence Ltd., Eland House,
11 High Street, Maidenhead, Berks. Telephone: 28539.

Revised 13th April, 1967.

gave 160+ bhp on Weber carburettors; while Phase IV gave 175+ bhp on fuel injection. (The 'Mike Spence' BRM Elans were built during 1967 and were of Phase 1 tune—approximately 20 were built.)

The best racing engines, in fact, were Cosworth/BRM hybrids, and Team Lotus fitted these in their Cortinas. Jim Clark and Graham Hill used them, and the 47s also had them in 1967–68. BRM's gas-flowing was superior to Cosworth's, as were their head work and camshafts, but their engine bottom end was almost too stiff with massive con-rods and

crankshaft and Mahle pistons. Cosworth, on the other hand, used Hepworth-Grandage pistons and their own rods and steel crankshaft. Steel cam followers were fitted instead of cast-iron, together with hardened oversize valves (both inlet and exhaust), steel cam caps, and steel main-bearing caps (hence the name 'all-steel' twin-cam). Capacity was always 1594 cc, to stay within the 1600 cc class limit, and the maximum achieved on Tecalemit-Jackson fuel injection was 175–180 bhp, with a rev limit of 8500 rpm. This was the ultimate development used in the Lotus 47s. The highest ever power output achieved with a

Left
By late 1980s standards, the prices look very reasonable indeed!

Below
The stance everyone remembers—Jim Clark in characteristic pose, at Brands Hatch in 1964, in a works Lotus-Cortina

A twin-cam engined Lotus 47, owned by Pat Thomas

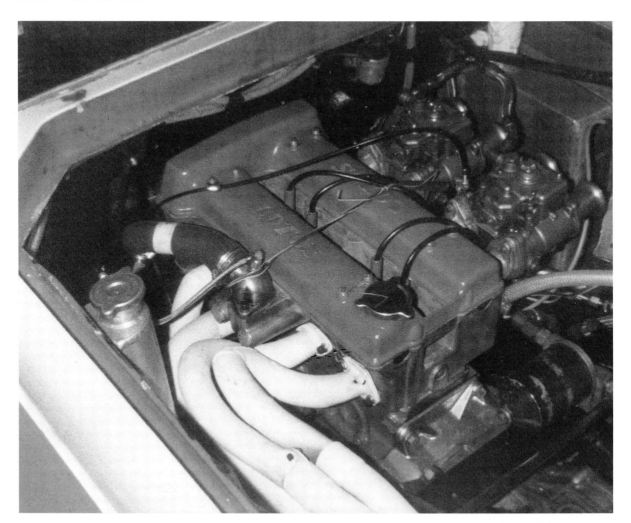

Above left
The Lotus 47 engine bay

Left
*UVW 924E—the Lotus-Cortina Mk II which won
the Gulf London rally of 1967. This car was
twin-cam powered, driven by Ove Andersson and
prepared by Ford-Boreham. The engine was fitted
with Tecalemit fuel injection*

Above
*The Tecalemit fuel-injection twin-cam engine
installation in a 1967 Lotus-Cortina Mk II*

Above
John Miles in his Elan 26R, at Crystal Palace, 6 August 1966. This car had a faired-in front bumper, perspex covers over the headlights, slightly flared bodywork over the wheels, suspension modifications, and J. A. Pearce wheels. In this guise, a 26R was usually unbeatable, and was almost banned from racing because of this! Even today, in historic sports-car races, a genuine 26R is hard to beat

Left
John Miles' epic drive at Brands Hatch, Easter 1966. His bonnet had been flapping about earlier in the race, so he stopped, Brian Muir pulled it off, and in spite of losing time, he managed to overtake Bernard Unett's Sunbeam Tiger on the last lap, to win

'normal' 1594 cc twin-cam was 185 bhp, whereas Brian Hart managed to extract around 200 bhp from an all-alloy-block twin-cam in 1974.

Many problems were encountered when fuel injection was fitted to the engine, especially with the earlier Lucas mechanical system which had no metering device; once it started up, everything was fine as fuel was being dumped in. However, as the revs dropped, neat fuel was still being dumped in, which was acceptable when on full bore, but disastrous when idling. The Tecalemit system was a little better but still unreliable, and was dropped in favour of Weber 45 DCOEs.

However, the Team Lotus 47s ended their days on T-J injection at Hethel in 1968. Another reason for dropping T-J early on was because it was too costly for production purposes on the 47s and Mk II Lotus-Cortinas. On 45 DCOEs, the 47s gave a maximum of 175 bhp at 8000 rpm, so power was only reduced by 5 bhp compared with injection.

All engines were dry-sumped, which meant that there was less drag, lubrication was assured at all times, there was no oil surge, and the oil tank, mounted in a convenient space, could receive cold air which cooled the oil. Both pressure and scavenge pumps were employed. On normal wet-sump engines, Cosworth high-pressure oil pumps were used, giving around 65 psi hot pressure. With these hybrids, the standard water pump and chain were retained.

One person who had many experiences with the 26R, 47 and Lotus-Cortina was John Miles, the highly-respected Lotus driver who applied meticulous attention to detail, and recently recalled his experiences. In 1966 he was driving a 26R Series II with a full BRM engine, which gave 135 bhp, as tested by Willments. A standard road crank was used, but with BRM rods and pistons. He won every race at the Goodwood Easter meeting. Willments then worked on the head, changing the cam profile and porting, and raising peak power to 148 bhp on Weber 40 DCOEs. Then the engine failed, and the bottom end was

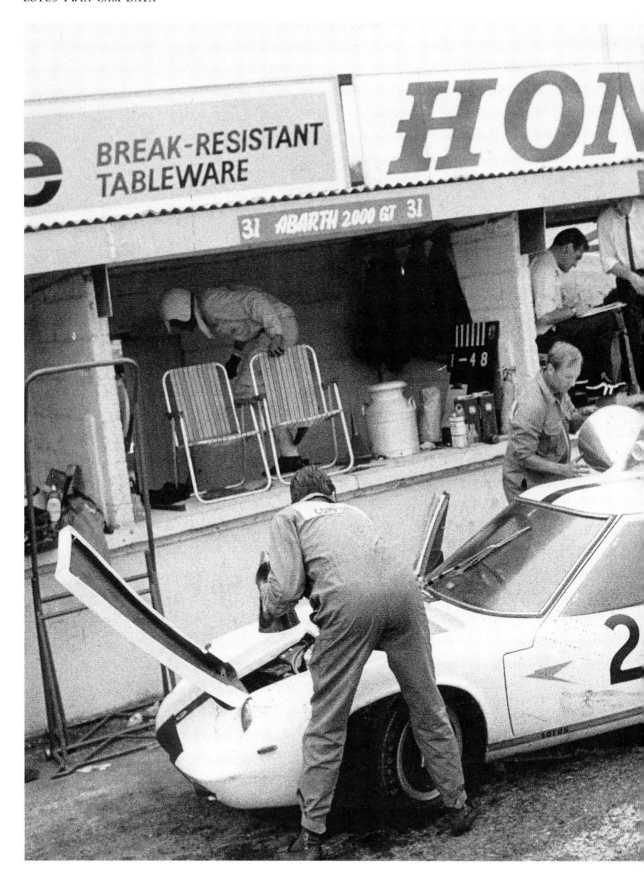

rebuilt with Cosworth rods and pistons, the head remaining the same but with larger 45 DCOEs being used. In the Oulton Park Gold Cup race, the road crank broke under the strain, so a steel one was fitted and John finished the season with no further trouble. The capacity was 1594 cc, maximum revs 7500 rpm, and maximum power was 155 bhp at 7000 rpm.

At the Gold Cup meeting, Colin Chapman invited John to try a Mk II Lotus-Cortina, which he drove in practice, but did not race; he was eventually enlisted to join Lotus Components to develop and drive the 47. His comments on fuel injection were that it was unreliable—indeed, one 47 caught fire in testing. He also drove the Cortinas on Lucas injection (which was even worse) and, in 1967, tried a fully-built BRM engine, although it did not produce the expected power output (175 bhp), more likely a true 160 bhp.

John is very sceptical about power outputs, although he acknowledges that testing procedures vary with different dynamometers and exhaust systems. His own logs, kept from Willment days, are meticulously presented. The so-called 160 bhp road engines, as advertised in the 1980s, must be queried, since John won everything in sight on a genuine 155 bhp, and a genuine 160 bhp becomes very difficult to drive on the road. John Miles, possibly more than anyone, knows what the true power outputs feel like, for his drives in the 47s are legendary.

The rally programme at Ford was engineered by two men, Bill Meade and Peter Ashcroft, who are still at Ford's Boreham facility today. They both recall that for the original Lotus-Cortina rally programme, the engines were built by BRM at Bourne, using their steel cranks, rods and Mahle pistons. (Henry Taylor, the competition manager, required a maximum oil consumption of 6 fl oz/hour, which is why BRM used Mahle pistons in an attempt to meet the requirement—he called the early blocks weepers, seepers and

This was John Miles' Lotus Components Lotus 47, painted white (the only colour available) at Brands Hatch for the 1967 BOAC 500-km meeting, where it won its class. The pit crew are Gordon Palmer, John Joyce, and David Lazenby; David looked after the 47 and, of course, also produced the single twin-cam engined Lotus Elite. The dry-sump oil tank in the 47 was in the front luggage compartment

Left
The Miles/Lotus 47 in action during the BOAC 500-km race of 1967. The high-level air intakes were added to help force cold air into the engine bay. Note that the private Lotus 47 (No. 32, behind the Ferrari) had no such intakes. The 47 was really a much-modified Europa, with cleaned up body, sitting on a different chassis, to accept a race-tuned twin-cam engine and a Hewland transaxle

Below left
The ultimate-tune Lotus 47, as driven by John Miles in Gold Leaf Team Lotus colours during 1968. The scene, once again, is the BOAC 500-km race. Note that since 1967 the front end had been cleaned up even further, and the air intakes had been abandoned

Above right
Mud, mud, glorious mud— a works Lotus-Cortina Mk II in the East African Safari of 1968

Right
The best way to prove the toughness of the Escort Twin Cam was to keep jumping it at the Bagshot testing grounds, until something broke, or the driver's nerve flew out of the window

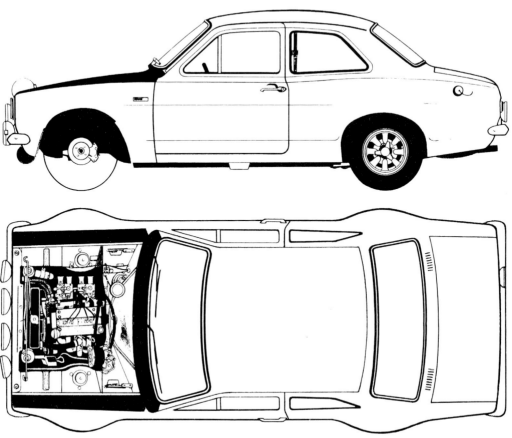

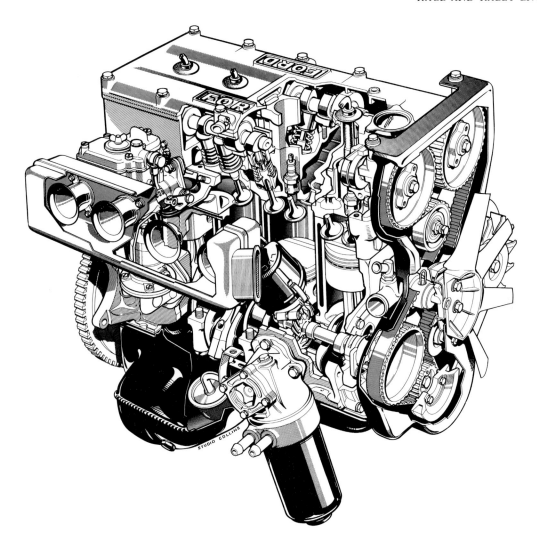

Above
Not to be confused with the Lotus twin-cam, this is the 16-valve Ford-Cosworth BDA engine, designed by Keith Duckworth's team and adopted for the Escort RS1600 and later high-performance Fords

Above left
One of the Alan Mann racing Twin Cams at the Zolder race circuit in 1968

Left
Ford's drawing of an Escort Twin Cam rally car clearly shows that the engine was installed at an angle to find clearance in the engine bay

pissers, on account of their porosity and ability to leak oil!) Although the development work was contracted to BRM by Ford, eventually the team engineer, Jack Welsh, became unhappy with them because of engine problems: 'Everything blew out around the bottom end. It was like girders in there, everything was overdone!' He looked for other suppliers, and one applicant was Vegantune of Spalding. This company supplied engines for the Cortina in 1966 and early 1967 (they were also building engines for Alan Mann). However, it was all short-lived, with Bill Meade and George Robinson soon having blinding rows about reliability, culminating in the decision that 'we can do better'—and they did!

From 1967 onwards, all of Ford's competition twin-cam engines were prepared in-house at Boreham, the standard unit arriving fully assembled from Hethel. The engines were stripped and reworked, with much attention being given to porting. A few were built with T-J fuel injection for the Mk II Cortina, but this was unsuccessful. (In fact, Boreham marketed T-J injection kits for private use, but only three sets were ever sold and the rest lay unused, until they

*The ultimate in Modsports cars—the Elan of
Kelvedon Motors, as raced in 1980*

were finally scrapped a few years ago.) With the
arrival of the Escort Twin Cam (code J25), the
engines first used 40 DCOEs, then 45s and finally
48s with L1 camshafts having 46/78/70/54 timing.

In the Escorts, the engines usually gave around
145 bhp, at best 160 bhp; lower than the racing
engines because reliability was essential. A few
problems were encountered: firstly, distributor
points bounce at over 6500 rpm was never really
eliminated, while oil leaks between backplate and
block were cured with cotton wool and paint—of
all things yellow road-lining paint, which just
happened to be lying around. A new front cover
was cast for the Escorts, to accept a larger water-
pump bearing, as the original was failing too
quickly because of the enormous side loads
imposed upon it by the heavy-duty alternator
needed to power the extra lights used on rallies.
The engine, however, was inherently reliable.

Other memorable twin-cam-powered cars built
at Boreham included two Ford Corsairs that were
entered in the 1964 Spa-Sofia-Liège rally. Both
started but neither finished, one being written off
after hitting a tractor on the first night. For Alan
Mann, there was a turbocharged twin-cam Escort
which was uncontrollable but which survived 200
yards on the test track before blowing up!

Ford never built any twin-cam Anglias. Such
cars were 'specials', built by private owners, but
several were raced professionally by drivers like
Graham Hill.

For today's users, the main criteria for a full-
race engine is to use a steel crankshaft, steel main
caps, Cosworth rods and pistons, a gas-flowed
and ported head, oversize valves, steel cam caps,
different camshafts (also with the cross oil drilling
taken out by the sprocket to prevent breakages), a
high-pressure fuel pump (Bendix or similar), and
a high-pressure oil pump or dry sump. The engine
should be fully balanced and blueprinted with
different carburation. The cost of assembling a
full-race engine will be around three times that of
a normal road-engine rebuild.

PART TWO

Engine rebuilding

1 General aspects of engine rebuilding

Before any work of this magnitude is even contemplated, it is essential to prepare, in your own mind, exactly what is to be done. Make sure you have a large, **clean** area in which to work, and do not forget that a stripped engine will take up at least four times the space of an assembled one. The next consideration is the most important of all—tools. No engine can be built with a motley collection of pre-war Whitworth specials. You must have the correct tool for the job, so if you have not got any of those listed below, buy them, or at least make sure you have access to them. Always buy the best that you can afford, for good tools will last a lifetime. The American Snap-On brand are the best; Britool are the British equivalent.

Note that the twin-cam engine is a British-designed engine, and therefore has all UNF and UNC nuts, studs and bolts. Spanner sizes are denoted AF. The engine does not have any other types of fixing.

Essential tools
Sockets: $\frac{7}{16}$, $\frac{1}{2}$, $\frac{9}{16}$, $\frac{5}{8}$, $\frac{11}{16}$, $\frac{3}{4}$, $\frac{13}{16}$, $\frac{7}{8}$ in., spark plug and stud extractor. All those are standard length, but you also need an extended $\frac{1}{2}$ in. socket. It is preferable to use a $\frac{3}{8}$ in. drive set rather than the larger $\frac{1}{2}$ in. drive.

Torque wrenches: two are required—0–40 lb ft and 20–110 lb ft type. You **cannot** rebuild an engine without these wrenches. If you use $\frac{3}{8}$ in. drive sockets, a $\frac{1}{2}$ in. to $\frac{3}{8}$ in. adaptor will also be required to allow their use with the torque wrenches.

Spanners: $\frac{7}{16}$, $\frac{1}{2}$, $\frac{9}{16}$, $\frac{5}{8}$, $\frac{15}{16}$ in. The combination type, i.e. with a ring at one end and open at the other, are the best.

Other tools: a small hammer, drifts, small circlip pliers, screwdrivers (large and small flat-bladed, and small Phillips), pliers, Mole grips (medium-to-large size), a small file, a valve-spring compressor, and a set of imperial size Allen keys.

Make sure you have a quantity of non-fluffy rags. Natural cotton is the only practical type, since man-made acetates and polyesters are not absorbent, and will dissolve in some solvents. Professional wipes can be bought from motor factors.

If AF sockets and spanners are difficult to obtain, the following metric sizes are equivalent:

$$11 \text{ mm} = \tfrac{7}{16} \text{ in.}$$
$$13 \text{ mm} = \tfrac{1}{2} \text{ in. (loose fit)}$$
$$14 \text{ mm} = \tfrac{9}{16} \text{ in. (tight fit)}$$
$$16 \text{ mm} = \tfrac{5}{8} \text{ in.}$$
$$17 \text{ mm} = \tfrac{11}{16} \text{ in. (tight fit)}$$
$$19 \text{ mm} = \tfrac{3}{4} \text{ in.}$$
$$22 \text{ mm} = \tfrac{7}{8} \text{ in.}$$
$$24 \text{ mm} = \tfrac{15}{16} \text{ in.}$$

If you have access to an engine stand then use it, as this will greatly facilitate the job. Have a bench or a large table to hand, spread with a clean cloth or newspaper, so that you have somewhere to put components as they are removed from the engine.

Removing ancillaries
With the engine out of the vehicle, it is preferable to clean off all the filth right away, although this is not essential, as every component will be cleaned scrupulously later on before reassembly—but it does make life easier. Use Jizer, Gunk or a similar compound, and hose off, or use a high-pressure, hot-water wash. If the carburettors, or dynamo or alternator are still in place, prevent them from becoming soaked by covering them with poly-

The engine from an Elan +2S130. Work on the engine will be easier if it is mounted on an engine stand

thene bags. Remove the engine to the bench or, if using a stand, undo the exhaust-side engine mounting (or bracket), and bolt the stand plate to the block at that point.

If any ancillaries are left on, remove them at this stage. Weber or Dellorto carburettors should be removed as an assembly with the metal backplate (if fitted) by undoing the eight nuts holding the Thackery washers. Then slide the carburettors off the studs; the breather pipe will slide out of the head at the same time. Strombergs are removed in the same way, but only six nuts hold them to the adaptor blocks. With the Strombergs out of the way, undo the eight nuts holding the adaptor blocks and balance pipe, and slide them off. The dynamo, or alternator, comes off next,

after undoing the adjuster bolt and the two bottom bracket bolts. Lift it away, together with the V-belt. Unclip the distributor cap and remove it with the HT leads. Remove the inlet-side engine mounting (if it is still fitted). The engine is now ready for strip-down.

One final point: if for any reason or application the exhaust manifold has been left on (i.e. original Elan S1, 2, or early 3, late-model T/C Europa cast manifold, or any racing application), this must be removed by undoing the eight brass nuts and pulling it away. Discard the four gaskets. On Federal engines, before removing the carburettors and cast-iron manifold, take off the cross-over pipes.

2 Engine strip-down

The strip-down sequence begins with removal and dismantling of the head, followed by the clutch, flywheel, fuel pump, oil pump, sump and front cover, and finishes with stripping the block assembly itself.

The cam cover is released by removing the eight $\frac{1}{4}$ in. UNF Nyloc nuts and metal and rubber/metal (called Senloc) washers. Discard both nuts and washers. Pull off the cam cover; if it is stuck fast, gently ease it upwards at the rear bridge piece near the oil filler cap by tapping a flat-bladed screwdriver through the gasket. Discard the cam-cover gasket and D-plugs (four on all engines except on the Europa, which has three).

Although it is not essential, some people feel happier if the engine is turned to TDC at this stage, the pulley notch being aligned with the TDC mark on the front cover. Number four cylinder inlet and exhaust camshaft lobes will then be pointing in towards each other.

Remove the sparking plugs and either keep or discard them, depending on their condition. Undo both camshaft-sprocket bolts and unwind the timing-chain tensioner by slackening the $\frac{5}{16}$ in. UNF Nyloc nut. Wind the tensioner thread back to its fullest extent with a flat-bladed screwdriver. Remove the sprocket bolts, together with their special washers, pull off the sprockets and allow the timing chain to drop down inside the front cover. (The exhaust-cam sprocket should have 'EX' etched or scribed on it; make sure it is different from the inlet-cam sprocket to start with—see later—and then mark it, if it has not been marked already.) Progressively release the inlet-camshaft retaining caps. When all five caps are undone (discard the $\frac{5}{16}$ in. UNF Nyloc nuts), remove them with the camshaft. (On the Europa, the alternator drive pulley comes off first—the

camshaft comes away with the oil seal on it.) Repeat for the exhaust camshaft.

If the cam bearings are to be retained, it is imperative that they are kept in their respective places—mark them meticulously, otherwise discard them. The inlet and exhaust camshafts are identical, but they must go back in the same bank. Then, with the aid of a valve grinding tool (valve 'sucker'), pull out the tappets (buckets) and shims on the inlet side. Repeat for the exhaust side. Mark them 'Inlet 1–4' and 'Exhaust 1–4' as appropriate, or if renewing them, discard the tappets and only mark the shims.

Undo the three bolts holding the head to the front cover ($\frac{5}{16}$ in. UNC) and then, with the torque wrench set at 100 lb ft, progressively release the ten head bolts—start in the middle of the head and work out to the ends. They will come loose with a loud crack. Withdraw the bolts and lift away the head by holding the inlet manifold and the thermostat housing. Discard the head gasket (inspect it first, if still intact, for any unknown blowing), the head-to-block rubber oil-drain tube, and the cork front-cover gasket.

With the head on a separate section of bench or table, remove the valves with a deep-headed valve-spring compressor that will reach well into the ports. Compress each spring in turn and remove the two valve collets, then release the compressor. Remove the top retainer, inner and outer valve springs, the bottom seat and the valve. Repeat this for all valves. Mark all eight valve sets if they are to be kept or discard the springs and valves if renewing, together with any broken or distorted valve-spring seats, retainers or collets.

Take off the timing-chain tensioner bracket pin and sprocket assembly. Remove the thermostat housing, discarding the gasket, and thermostat.

Left
*Undoing the cam cover—
note that the water elbow
on this engine has been
broken off, and the broken
temperature sender unit is
also the wrong way round*

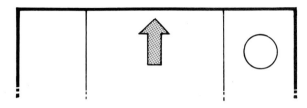

Left
*If the cam cover sticks, lift
it at the rear bridge piece*

Left
Removing the D-plugs

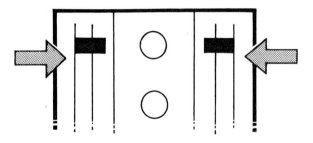

Left
*Number four inlet and
camshaft lobes should point
towards each other*

69

Undoing the camshaft sprockets

Removing the sprockets, and allowing the chain to fall down behind the front cover

Undoing the cam caps

Lifting out the camshafts

Removing the tappets (cam followers) with the aid of a valve grinding tool

Undoing the head and front-cover bolts

Removing the head bolts

Lifting off the cylinder head

The block assembly, after the head has been removed

Next release the oil-breather elbow or grommet; the elbow pulls out, but the grommet will be rock hard and will require breaking and pulling away with long-nosed pliers. Do not worry if it falls into the hole as one can go to the head-to-block breather-tube hole and fish the bits out—several may be in there already!

Inspect the various studs, (cam cover, inlet and exhaust), and if any are damaged, remove them, either with a stud extractor, or two nuts locked together. The cam-cover studs usually suffer from waisted threads, and the exhaust studs become damaged when the manifolds are forced on and off. At this stage, the head is basically bare.

Return to the block assembly. Undo the clutch cover (six $\frac{5}{16}$ in. UNC bolts) and remove it together with the plate (inspect both and discard if unserviceable). With a bar or a large screwdriver placed across two of the flywheel dowels, undo the crankshaft pulley bolt, and remove it, together with its thick washer. Pull off the pulley—if it is stuck, use two screwdrivers to gently work it off. Remove the water-pump pulley hub and fan, if fitted (four $\frac{1}{4}$ in. UNC bolts). At the flywheel, tap back the lock tabs (four-bolt type only) and, as before, prevent it turning with a bar across two dowels and undo the four or six bolts. Pull the flywheel assembly off the crankshaft. Take off the mechanical fuel pump (two $\frac{5}{16}$ in. UNC bolts) and discard the packing block. Remove the oil filter, using a chain wrench to grip the canister, or by undoing the central bolt on the earlier, renewable-paper-element type. Then release the oil-pump assembly (three $\frac{5}{16}$ in. UNC bolts) and pull it away, twisting it slightly to clear the helical gear; discard the gasket. Slacken the distributor clamp and withdraw the distributor, again twisting it to free it from the helical gear. Unscrew the $\frac{1}{4}$ in. UNC bolt holding the clamp base plate and remove the plate.

Now turn the block assembly upside down—the remains of oil and water will run out—and take off the sump ($\frac{1}{4}$ in. UNC set screws). When all the screws have been removed, gently tap off the sump and discard the gaskets and cork, rubber or rope seals around the front cover and rear oil-seal housing (six-bolt type only) or around the crank (four-bolt type). Remove the rear oil-seal housing (four $\frac{5}{16}$ in. UNC bolts) complete with seal (six-bolt type only).

Undo the front-cover bolts – $\frac{1}{4}$ in. UNC into the block, with one $\frac{5}{16}$ in. UNC and $\frac{1}{4}$ in. UNF bolts and Nyloc nuts—and very carefully pull away the front-cover/water-pump assembly. If this is stuck, due to corrosion of the water pump or too much sealant, carefully tap around the water-pump area using a soft drift. Do not hammer it, as this will distort the backplate and, in some cases, crack it. Remove the chain (if split-linked discard this immediately) and the crankshaft oil slinger. Note that there is no gasket between the front cover and backplate. Bend back the lock tab on the jackshaft sprocket, and unscrew the two $\frac{5}{16}$ in. UNC bolts by placing a drift in the sprocket to prevent it turning. Then remove the sprocket. Release the $\frac{1}{4}$ in. set screw holding the backplate and gently tap the plate from the block face; discard the gasket.

Undo the jackshaft's 'horse shoe' retaining plate (two $\frac{1}{4}$ in. UNC set screws) and withdraw the jackshaft. (For those unfamiliar with the term 'jackshaft', in this instance it is the camshaft from the standard 1500/1600 overhead-valve Ford engine; in the Lotus application it becomes an auxiliary shaft driving only the oil and fuel pumps and the distributor.)

Remove the oil pick-up pipe and strainer on the four-bolt crank by undoing the retaining nut on the cranked pipe and pulling the assembly out of the block; on the six-bolt version remove the oil strainer from its tube by bending back the three tags and pulling it away, then slide a snug-fitting bolt into the end of the tube to prevent it being crushed when you grip it with a pair of Mole grips. Tap against these to free the tube from the block. Repeat for the other tube.

Make sure that the big-end and main caps are marked 1–4 and 1–5 respectively, and undo numbers one and four big-end bolts, using a torque wrench. Remove each cap by replacing the bolts in it and using them as levers to lift it from the locating dowels. Rotate the crankshaft and repeat for caps two and three. Using the torque wrench, progressively release the crankshaft main caps, working from the centre cap out to the ends. Remove all five caps and lift out the crankshaft—if bearings are to be retained, mark them carefully. Collect the half-moon thrust washers from the centre main journal. Then push out the piston assemblies; if they are tight because of a bore ridge, gently tap them out with a wooden drift. Mark the bearings if they are to be kept.

Finally, remove the water-jacket core plugs, two on the exhaust side and one at the rear, using a suitable drift. Knock in one side and pivot the plug about its centre. Pull them out with long-nosed pliers. In most cases, a build-up of rust and

Undoing the clutch cover

After removing the clutch assembly, the flywheel is removed by using a long bar, anchored against a steady bar

Removing the front pulley, with the aid of a small, two-legged puller

Removing the front hub pulley

Removing the fuel pump, followed by the oil pump, distributor, and engine mountings

Removing the sump

Pulling away the rear oil seal and its housing

Loosening the front cover

Gently prising the front-cover/water-pump assembly from the backplate

With the front cover
removed, this shows the
chain and jackshaft
sprocket

After knocking back the
lock tabs, undo the
jackshaft sprocket

Releasing the backplate
retaining screw, and
removing the plate

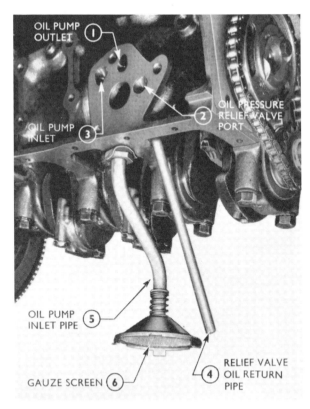

OIL PUMP OUTLET ①

OIL PRESSURE RELIEF VALVE PORT ②

OIL PUMP INLET ③

OIL PUMP INLET PIPE ⑤

GAUZE SCREEN ⑥

RELIEF VALVE OIL RETURN PIPE ④

Above left
After knocking back the jackshaft retaining-plate lock tabs, remove the shaft

Above
The four-bolt engine's oil pick-up and drain tubes

Left
Removing the oil pick-up and drain tubes (see text); these are to be discarded. Note the flattening of the tubes, caused by a previous, careless rebuilder. Use Mole grips, locked tightly around the tubes, and turn them from side to side, then pull upwards

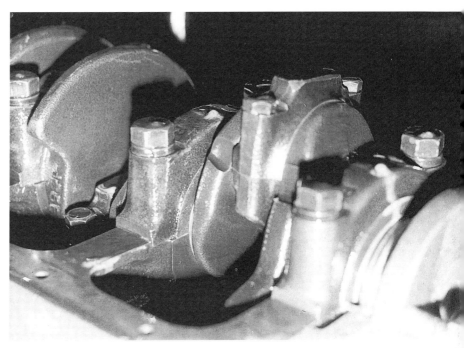

Above and above right
The round-shouldered main-bearing caps of the four-bolt engine, as opposed to the square-shouldered caps of the six-bolt engine. Note the thin L-type connecting rods with 5/16 in. bolts used with the four-bolt crank, as opposed to the 3/8 in. bolts of the six-bolt type

Right
Undoing the main-cap bolts

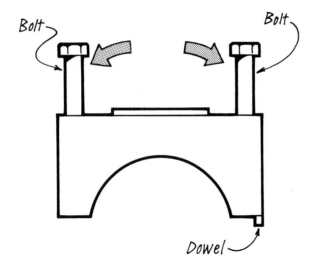

Use the bolts to lever the
bearing cap free

After undoing the big-end
bolts, use the bolts as levers
and tap the cap gently to
release it from its locating
dowels

Lifting out the crankshaft
and removing the two
thrust washers

The block, showing piston assemblies still in place. All main and big-end bearings show signs of scoring and wear

With the block on end, push the piston assemblies out from the top

Removing core plugs by knocking one edge into the block to turn it on its axis. Then prise, or pull, it out

Change core plugs regularly. This one was paper thin, with only an accumulation of sludge and rust holding it together

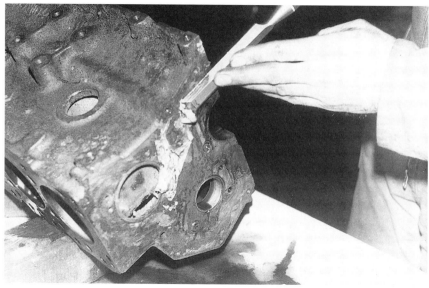

After removing the oil-gallery plugs, scrape off the remnants of gaskets, prior to machining, and a thorough degreasing and washing

A sintered bronze bush spigot bearing for the four-bolt crankshaft (right), and a needle-roller bearing for the six-bolt crank (left)

The end of a four-bolt crankshaft, showing the sintered bronze bush and the flywheel locating dowel

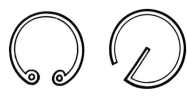

Gudgeon pin clips

Water-pump bearing clip

Pulling off the water-pump hub, using a small, two-legged puller. After pulling out the bearing retainer clip, heat the cover or immerse it in boiling water, and extract the bearing, using a press and a suitable mandrel. The bearing comes away complete with seals and impellor. Remove the impellor housing by pulling it out of the cover

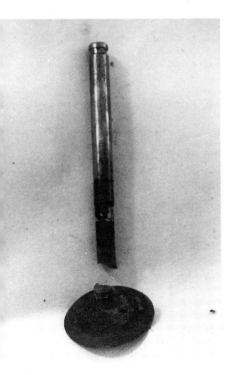

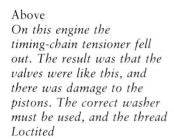

Above
On this engine the timing-chain tensioner fell out. The result was that the valves were like this, and there was damage to the pistons. The correct washer must be used, and the thread Loctited

Above right and right
An excessively-loose chain resulted in serious wear on the damper and cover on the opposite side. This should never be allowed to happen—the noise must have been deafening!

Right
Method of removing the timing-chain tensioner thread

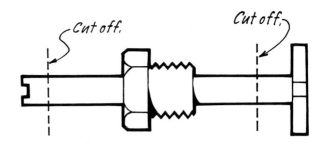

sediment is all that will be holding in the plug. Undo the brass drain plug (or tap) and the three oil-gallery plugs, using an Allen key. For rebuild purposes, the block now can be regarded as completely bare, save for the jackshaft bearings, which will be dealt with later.

The few sub-assemblies on twin-cams can be dealt with separately, but (for continuity's sake) while stripping the engine carry out the following, if found to be necessary. The rear oil seal (six-bolt) can be tapped out from the reverse shouldered face using a drift and tapping at opposite sides of the seal; sometimes, even placing the aluminium housing in boiling water for a few moments will allow the seal to be pushed out with the thumbs. The starter ring gear on the flywheel can be cut between two teeth with a hacksaw, then split with a cold chisel so that it falls away.

The spigot bearing on some transaxle installations (Europa) and the five-speed +2S130 model locates in the flywheel, and can be tapped out using a drift to match the outside diameter. The spigot bearing on the six-bolt crankshaft and for most four-speed cars, i.e. all Elans and +2s, sits in the end of the crankshaft. It can be removed by packing the remainder of the recess with grease and hammering a close-fitting drift (a clutch-plate alignment tool is ideal) into the bearing to force the grease round behind it. The hydraulic pressure created should push the bearing out, although several attempts may be required before this is achieved. The early type of bearing, which was a phosphor-bronze bush, was used solely in the four-bolt crankshaft, and is removed in the same way.

Pistons can be separated from the connecting rods by removing the circlips or wire clips with circlip pliers or needle-nosed pliers respectively, and pushing the gudgeon pin through the rod until the piston is free. To remove the piston rings pull their ends apart and slide them from the piston. The small-end bush can be extracted with a press, using a suitable mandrel.

The front-cover assembly is the largest sub-assembly and is stripped in the following manner. If not already removed, unscrew the tensioner nut and take it off together with the spring and plunger sleeve. Pull off the water-pump pulley with a small hub puller. Always use a puller—never try to drive it off, as you may damage the cover. Remove the wire bearing clip with long-nosed pliers and immerse the cover in boiling water for a few moments. Support the cover and press the water-pump bearing out, using a mandrel (such as a socket) that matches the bearing's outside diameter. The bearing will come away easily with its seal, slinger and impellor. Remove the alloy ring with its two rubber O-rings and discard the lot. Do not drive the bearing out cold with a hammer, as it will be forced out, taking aluminium from its housing with it. This results in a sloppy fit for successive bearings, and water-pump leaks. The front-cover oil seal can be pushed out by hand while the cover is still hot. If it will not move, drift it out by tapping at opposite points on its circumference, supporting the cover around the seal. To finish stripping the cover, use a large flat-bladed screwdriver to release the two $\frac{1}{4}$ in. UNC screws that hold the timing-chain damper (slipper) in place.

If the crankshaft sprocket has to be removed because it is damaged, it must be pressed off by using a bearing plate (or two even supports such as steel bars) under the sprocket. Screw in the pulley bolt and press down on the bolt, supporting the crankshaft at the same time. Never hit the crankshaft with a hammer, as unseen stress or fracture lines may occur, with disastrous results later on. The timing-chain tensioner sprocket can be removed from its brass carrier by undoing the flat-headed pivot bolt. The timing-chain tensioner assembly thread is removed from the nut, either by cutting off the washer or by cutting off the slotted end after removing the $\frac{5}{16}$ in. UNF Nyloc nut, deburring and undoing through the nut.

By this time the engine will have been reduced to its component parts, and the process of checking for wear and damaged components begins, together with cleaning, ready for any necessary machining and final assembly. Things can go wrong on a strip-down, so always work slowly and carefully, rather than charging ahead and tearing everything off, breaking studs here and there, and failing to spot pieces of metal floating around the engine or the remains of a nut bouncing into the head or piston. So, while in the process of stripping down an engine, and indeed when it is stripped, reassemble various parts to measure wear. All the fits and clearances are given in the tables at the end of the book, but nine times out of ten these will not be needed, because most defects will be obvious. Alternatively, the engine may be being rebuilt because of a known problem.

3 Checking for wear, machining and cleaning

Among the obvious signs of wear are 'wet' oil marks and heavily-coked, wet sludge around the exhaust ports which indicate that the engine is burning oil heavily, so look for worn rings and valve guides. Deep scores or grooves in the camshaft bearings may be caused by dirt or swarf from previous rebuilds, or by sandblasting. If in this condition, they should be discarded. Cams may be heavily scored as well. Main and big-end bearings that are heavily scored or worn to the copper should also be discarded. Look for heavily-scored pistons and ridged cylinder bores. Prior to strip-down, the water-pump bearing may be rumbling or rattling, or the hub may be loose.

Slip the valves back in, one by one, without the springs, then pull each valve head away from its seat and rock it in the guide. It will be obvious if the clearance is too large. Check the valve for bad seating and pitting. Check the seat (insert) itself; with standard camshafts, i.e. those that have not been reprofiled in any way, if the tappet shim is less than 0.075 in. thick new inserts must be fitted. Check the head face for corrosion around the waterways again, this should be obvious. Has the corrosion travelled too far toward the combustion chamber? Check the head face for distortion, using a straight edge. Examine the front cover for distortion and corrosion around the water-pump area. Check the block for rebore, and ridging in the bores. Inspect the crankshaft for scoring on the journals—you may have to have it reground. It will be obvious from the state of the clutch plate whether it is worn or oil-soaked because of a leaking rear main oil seal. The starter ring gear should be checked for smashed or missing teeth.

These are all items which anybody with a little knowledge can see for himself; above all, if in any

doubt, seek professional guidance. When the course of action has been decided upon, make a list of all the necessary parts and machining to be done and come to terms with the cost of the operation. Never skimp on parts, and, where appropriate, renew with genuine Lotus parts only—as we have seen, 90 per cent were Lotus-drawn anyway. After spending 40–50 hours on a rebuild, the last thing anyone wants is a wrecked engine caused by cheap parts or incompetent machining.

The finer points of measurement can either be done by yourself, provided the proper gauges are available and used correctly, or be left to the professional (which is usually cheaper and quicker in the long run).

Wear in the valve guides and seats is obvious and has been mentioned already, however, the clearance of the tappet in the tappet sleeve should be checked. Use a wire gauge, i.e. a wire of predetermined thickness used in the same way as a feeler gauge. As with the piston-to-bore clearance, some people measure the gap with a feeler gauge. This is wrong, since it will not measure the true gap, for the feeler gauge becomes the tangent to the piston. The usual method is to use a bore gauge which is inserted into the bore (either the tappet sleeve or cylinder bore) and the diameter is measured at several points for ovality. The tappet, or piston, is measured using a micrometer, again in several places to check for ovality. The difference between the mean diameters of the bore and tappet, or piston, gives the true clearance figure. By comparing this with the fits and clearances tables, you can see whether the items are within limits, or not.

The crankshaft journals should be checked for ovality with a micrometer, taking measurements

Above left and left
When oil escapes down the valve guides, it leaves this characteristic oil trace at the ports. New guides and valves are needed

Left
One cause of a massive oil leak—a squashed head-to-block rubber. This must always be located properly

Sand blasting the head caused this! It destroyed the camshaft and its bearings because sand was carried round in the oil. The crankshaft and its bearings were also in the same state

The fuel pump, placed incorrectly, gouged the jackshaft. Naturally, this seized the engine

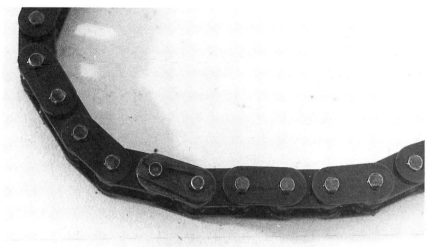

Never use a split-linked chain. If the link comes off, everything stops

Time for a new chain—the tensioner is wound in too far

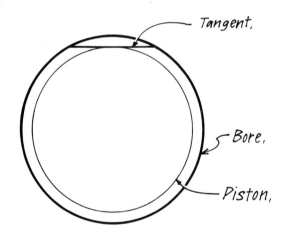

A feeler gauge gives an incorrect measurement when checking piston-to-bore clearance

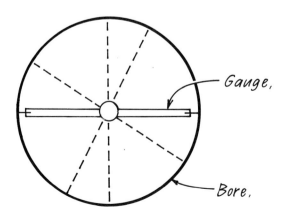

Use a bore gauge to check for ovality, taking measurements at several points

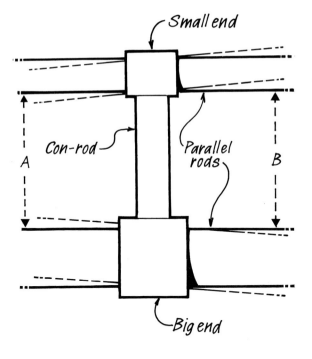

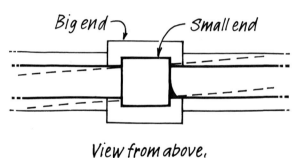

View from above.

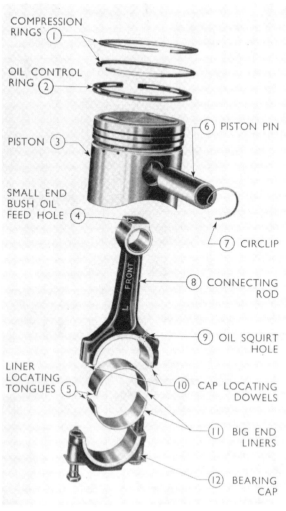

① COMPRESSION RINGS

② OIL CONTROL RING

③ PISTON

④ SMALL END BUSH OIL FEED HOLE

⑤ LINER LOCATING TONGUES

⑥ PISTON PIN

⑦ CIRCLIP

⑧ CONNECTING ROD

⑨ OIL SQUIRT HOLE

⑩ CAP LOCATING DOWELS

⑪ BIG END LINERS

⑫ BEARING CAP

Con-rods are checked for distortion with parallel bars inserted through the small-end and big-end bores. If the rod is straight, distance 'A' will equal distance 'B'. Twist can be seen by looking down at the rods from directly above.

The early L-type connecting rod and an A-type piston. This assembly has much smaller connecting-rod bolts than the later C-type

at several points on each journal, and of course, the limits of the journals themselves. Connecting rods can be checked for bearing ovality by bolting each cap to its respective rod and measuring its bore with a bore gauge or internal micrometer. A bent or twisted con-rod is usually obvious when compared to a straight (new) one, but it can be measured using parallel bars of correct diameter passed through the big-end and small-end, with no bearings in place. If the con-rod is straight, the distance between the bars will be the same on each side of the rod; if it is bent, the distances will vary. If the rod is twisted, the rods will lie at an angle to each other when viewed from above. If a con-rod is bent or twisted, or has an oval bore, a new one or set must be used; under no circumstances attempt to straighten a bent rod, as any stresses caused will ultimately result in a fracture. C-type rods will never bend of their own accord; only a severe disaster will bend a rod. In the unlikely event that you come across L-type rods, they should be replaced immediately by the C-type, regardless of their condition. Never mix the two types in an engine.

The clearance between the piston rings and their grooves can be measured with a feeler gauge. Very worn rings will move up and down easily in the groove, causing premature groove wear, so check very carefully for this if the pistons are to be retained.

Small-end bushes can be checked for wear by holding the piston firmly in one hand and trying to rock it on the small-end bush. The piston must not be allowed to slide along the bush, which will give the impression of wear. Inspect the gudgeon pin for signs of 'stepping' where it passes through the bush, and also check the fit of the pin in the piston. This should be a sliding push-fit; if it rattles around, a new piston (set) must be used. Also check the piston/pin circlip groove—if you find any damage, the piston must be replaced, since a circlip coming adrift will cause untold damage to the piston and the bore.

Examine the camshafts and jackshaft for bearing-surface scoring, and check the lobe pattern on the camshafts. There should be no irregular wear, pitting or pieces broken off. Look for excessive wear on the jackshaft's helical gear drive to the oil pump and distributor, and make sure that the lobe for the fuel-pump drive is in good order. Check the tappets for any pitting where the surface hardness may have worn off, and if you find any discard them, as eventually this will lead to the tappets breaking up. Check all sprockets for irregular wear or tooth damage, replacing them as necessary, and check the brass carrier to make sure the timing-chain sprocket is not bent or the pin sleeve worn away. The pin itself must not be stepped or grooved. Once everything has been checked thoroughly, any machining or rectification can be carried out.

Overhauling the cylinder head

It is not necessary to remove all the studs, but it is more professional to do so, particularly as most of them will need replacing anyway. All studs will have to be removed if the head-bolt faces have gouged the head, through continued over-tightening on distorted or incorrect washers.

Most professional machinists use argon-arc, low-temperature aluminium welding to rectify any cracks, combustion-chamber damage or corroded waterways (new advances in welding technology mean that very little or no distortion occurs—this is vital when working on very old and much-skimmed heads, where severe distortion and subsequent skimming would destroy a head). This operation is not for the home builder to attempt in any way.

If the tappet (cam-follower) sleeves are to be replaced, two diametrically-opposite grooves should be cut down their length from the scallops (cut-outs) and each sleeve should be split with a sharp cold chisel. If any burrs are thrown up on the aluminium, these must be removed, the head heated uniformly to 150 degrees Celsius in an oven, and the new sleeve inserted, using a mandrel to bear down evenly on the outside diameter of the sleeve. When in situ and cold, the sleeve must be machined to the clearances given; then the scallops should be recut and deburred. Do not over-machine, otherwise the new tappets will rattle around in the same way as did the old. New tappets must be fitted with the new sleeves and, ideally, each individual sleeve should be machined to match its tappet—effectively blueprinted. In theory, all the tappets are the same and should not affect sleeve machining; however, they may vary by a few tenths of a thousandth of an inch.

The inlet and exhaust valve guides are different and must be fitted in their respective banks. First of all it pays to remove any heavy build-up of carbon oil sludge around the tips of the guides—usually only on the exhaust side—with a sharp scraper, but do not score the head. Then heat the head uniformly to 150 degrees Celsius and, from

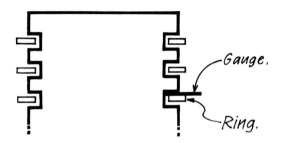

Measuring piston-to-ring clearance

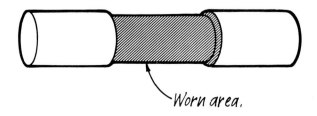

Check for gudgeon-pin wear

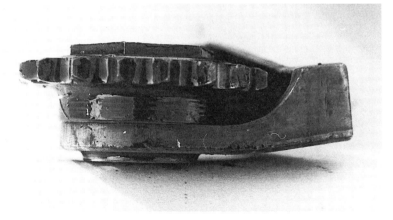

Left and below left Irregular and excessive wear on sprocket teeth. The only answer is to fit new components

An excessively-worn timing-chain pivot pin

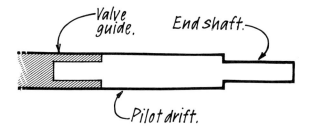

A pilot drift with the same outside diameter as the valve guide is needed to remove it

The head, after heating, shows guides and seats removed

the valve side, use a pilot drift to tap the guide and its circlip into the tappet-sleeve bore. By removing the excess carbon first, you will prevent muck being dragged up the guide bore and damaging the aluminium. Under no circumstances must the guide be driven out cold, as the bore will be severely damaged. The guide bore must be spotlessly clean, and the new guide should be inserted with a new circlip already fitted to it; with the head still at 150 degrees Celsius, push the guide in until the circlip is heard to snap into the head recess. Do not continue, as you may push the guide through the circlip. When cold, if the guide is loose or in any way lying suspect in the head, it must be removed and a guide with an oversize outside diameter installed. This entails reaming the head bore to the correct size and repeating the fitting process. The interference fit of all guides in the head is 0.0005–0.0015 in. (0.0127–0.0381 mm).

The guides must be reamed when cold in situ to give the required valve-stem clearance. As we have seen, this operation is critical, and any over-reaming will result in no improvement in oil control at all. Indeed, many people make it worse. New valves should always be fitted to new guides because of irregular valve-stem wear; as with the tappets, ream each guide to suit each valve.

The final operation is to recut the valve seat (insert)—either the existing seat or a new one—to ensure the seat is concentric with the stem bore. This operation is essential, since there could be machining variations in the old and new guides—for example, the internal diameter may be biased towards one side—and, of course, a wear pattern will already have become established in an old guide. An uncut seat would result in the valve not sealing, causing a loss of compression. Valve seats should be renewed if they are badly pitted or ridged and cannot be recut to the correct angle of 45 degrees without setting the seat face so far down in the head that the valve protrudes too far upwards and needs too thin a tappet shim to gain the correct clearance. To remove the seats, carefully drill through the angle at diametrically-opposite points, then use a small, sharp cold chisel to split the insert and allow removal. Only the seat must be touched, not the head.

The seat recess in the head must be spotlessly clean and have no burrs. Before fitting the new seat, the head must be heated to 180 degrees Celsius (not exceeding 200 degrees Celsius) and, ideally, the insert should be chilled in a freezer (−18 degrees Celsius). Lotus say dry ice (solid carbon dioxide) should be used to lower the seat's temperature to −80 degrees Celsius, but realistically nobody ever has dry ice in their homes! At these extremes of temperature, the insert will literally fall into place and is held square while the temperature returns to normal. Usually, however, the insert is pressed in and allowed to cool naturally. It is essential that the seat is sitting squarely in its recess. If it is not, it must be removed and a new one fitted properly. If there is any looseness or incorrect seating, oversize seats are available, and the head must be machined to accept these. The seats are then recut; many machine shops that do this regularly have a dummy valve/camshaft set-up so that the seats can be cut to the required depth to allow duplication of the original shimming. From 1967 virtually all heads left the factory in the 0.100–0.120 in. shim thickness range. This allows around three seat recuts from new before the 0.060 in. shim limit is reached. As with the guides, if the seat is over-cut for any reason, the exercise becomes pointless with shims in the 0.060–0.070 in. range, as effectively there is no further to go. The interference fit of all inserts in the head is 0.0025–0.0045 in. (0.0521–0.0114 mm).

Any stud-hole threads that have been damaged can either be retapped or fitted with a Helicoil (a steel insert which is screwed into the hole and which has a reverse thread, so that when the stud is inserted the Helicoil thread will automatically tighten and can never come out). Broken studs can have a pilot hole drilled in them and be removed with a stud extractor—a little local heat may be required. The head-bolt faces can be tidied up if required by spot facing each one. Never machine the top of the head or the cam-cover face to tidy up the bolt-head faces. The line-bore of the camshaft would be lost as the cam caps would sit lower and the camshafts would not turn.

Finally, if required, the head should be machined (skimmed) flat and true; for this, it is clamped on a bed and is fly cut. Machines vary as to the coarseness of cut, but a fine cut is essential. The depth can be controlled down to 0.001 in.

Overhauling the cylinder block

Usually, the main machining needed on the block is a rebore, because of scored or ridged bores, or simply because the clearance has become excessive due to normal wear. A rebore is a precision operation, the block being clamped on to a 'table' and the borer, using tungsten-carbide cutters,

Left
Reaming the guides in situ—the dark staining on the head is a result of dipping in a hot solvent-degreasant bath prior to being washed off

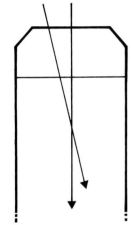

Above
In an old valve guide, the wear pattern may be at an angle

Right
Fitting the valve seats

The block being bored

The block, after being bored and stepped, ready to receive its liners. This block already had 0·040 in. oversize bores, and could not be bored further; hence the need for liners to return the block dimensions to standard

The liners, ready to be fitted

working its way down each bore.

Sleeving the block is done in the same way. If for example, a block is being prepared for road use and is already bored 0.040 in. oversize, on no account must it be bored any further, particularly if it is a Type LB block. In this situation, sleeves are used to return the bores to the standard diameter, and in this way many overbored blocks can be salvaged. Indeed, by using sleeves, blocks can remain in use *ad infinitum*. When fitting a sleeve, the block bore is opened out to the diameter of the sleeve, then a recess is cut and the sleeve is pressed in. Ovality is checked, and finally the top surface is faced, once again leaving a block ready to accept standard pistons.

If the bores are in good order, a light hone will be necessary to break the glaze, and to allow new piston rings to bed-in more easily. This is done using the same machine as for boring, but the attachment utilizes carborundum stones instead of tungsten-carbide cutters. This is also a precision operation. Many people use a piece of production paper (glasspaper or emery paper) on their fingers to 'score' the bores, or use 'flap' wheels and an electric drill. This may help slightly, but is not at all as effective as the professional operation.

Line-boring of the block is not a normal operation but must be mentioned here in case, on stripping down, a main cap breaks in half or the crankshaft, when bolted down, goes solid across one or more main caps. The line-bore is the original machining operation whereby the caps and block face are machined as one to create a true in-line diameter, allowing the crankshaft, with its respective bearings, to run freely. If this bore is distorted or damaged in any way, the crankshaft will not turn, and the line-bore must be re-established, with the true centre-line left undisturbed. This is achieved by milling, say, 0.005 in. off the main caps (and the 'odd' one) and 0.005 in. off the block locating faces, then bolting the caps down in their correct order to the correct torque setting, clamping the block assembly so that it is true and running the line borer through to recut the new diameter. Again, tungsten-carbide cutters are used.

This procedure must be carried out when all-steel caps are fitted for racing or, indeed, for road use. (The head should be treated in exactly the same way if the camshaft line-bore is out and one or both camshafts begin to bind when being tightened down.)

The jackshaft bearings should be pressed out, their bores cleaned thoroughly, and the new bearings pressed in. Usually, these bearings require no attention, being standard Ford items, but occasionally they may require reaming to suit the jackshaft diameter.

Finally, as with the head, Helicoiling any damaged threads and skimming (if required) completes the block machining.

Connecting rods usually cause no trouble, and unless there is a known problem (i.e. a bent rod or bearing ovality), the only necessary operation may be the replacement of the small-end bushes. These are pressed out, new ones pressed in and the oil hole drilled in each. Then the bushes must be reamed or honed to match the individual gudgeon pins.

Flywheel

Ideally, check the total run-out of the flywheel while it is still bolted to the crankshaft at the strip-down stage, using a dial gauge. Otherwise, mount the rear face of the flywheel on a mandrel after removing it from the crankshaft, again, using a dial gauge to measure the run-out. If this is excessive, the flywheel must be surface-ground to the correct limits. Surface grinding is also essential if the flywheel has been heavily scored or ridged by the rivets of a badly-worn clutch plate. If this is not done, the life of the new clutch plate will be severely reduced.

If a new starter ring gear is to be fitted, it should be heated gently to 300 degrees Celsius by playing a gas torch around the circumference, then placed on the flywheel and held there until it has contracted and gripped. It is imperative that the ring is not overheated, as the temper will be lost and the 'softened' teeth will have a short life. The ring must be located squarely and be allowed to cool naturally—do not quench it with water. Most important of all, check that the chamfers of the teeth leading edges face in the normal direction of rotation. Putting the ring on the wrong way round will ultimately ruin it and the Bendix drive of the starter motor.

Crankshaft

Machining of the crankshaft is confined to regrinding or polishing the journals. There are four reasons why regrinding may be necessary: oval journals, general wear, scoring by grit or excessively-worn bearings, and finally if the engine has been standing for years with old, acidic

Inserting the liners, using a press. Then they must be checked for ovality and, finally, the block/liner face skimmed flush

Honing the bores, where a rebore is not considered necessary

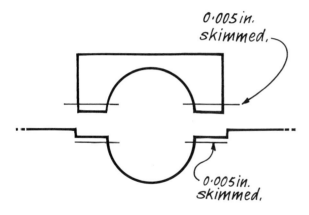

0·005 in.
skimmed.

0·005 in.
skimmed.

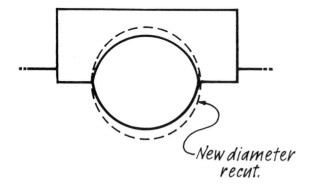

New diameter
recut.

When line-boring, material is skimmed from both caps and block. Then the bore is recut on the original centre-line

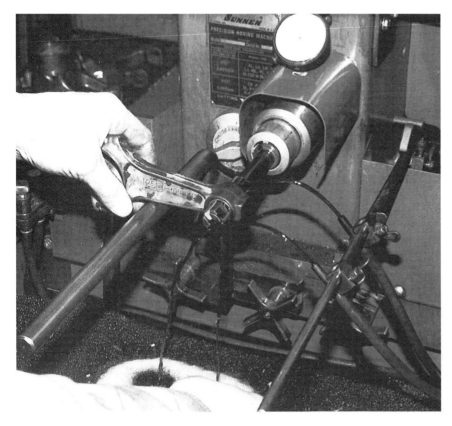

Reaming the small-end bush

99

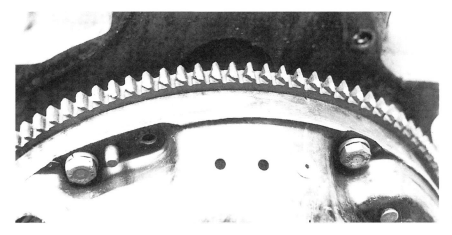

A seriously smashed starter ring gear

A crankshaft on the grinding machine

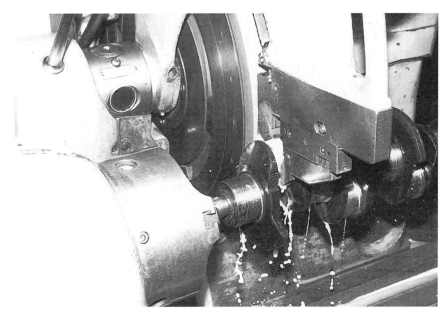

The grinding wheel in action. After this, preserving oil is smeared on the journals to prevent rust forming

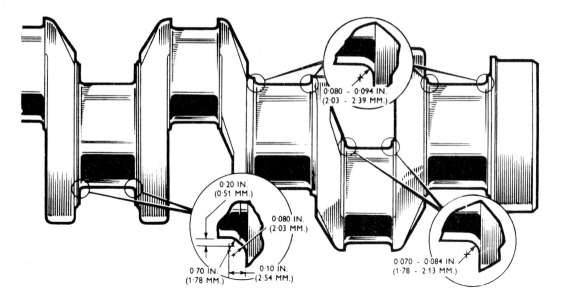

Above
This official Lotus drawing shows the fillet radii on the main and big-end journals of the twin-cam crankshaft

Below
Crankshaft journals being polished, using only these special tongs

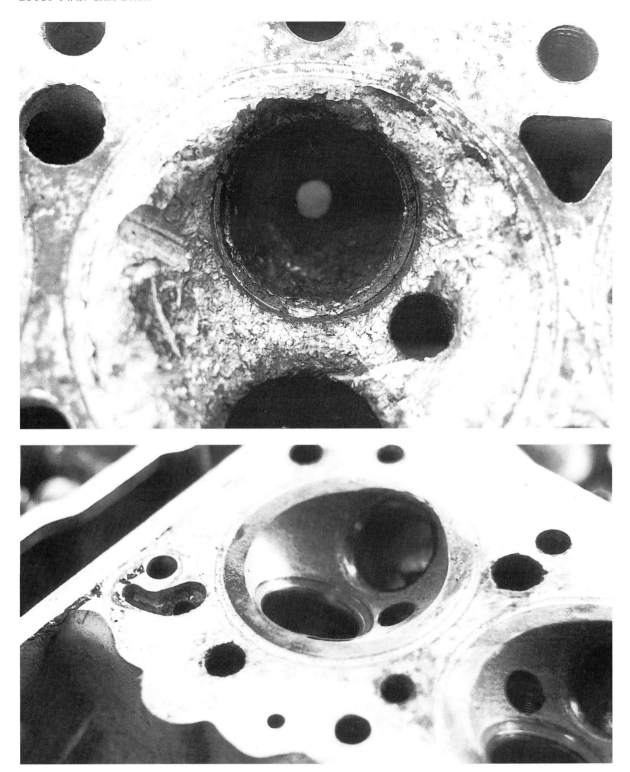

Top
The exhaust-valve seat fell out, making this cylinder head scrap—a typical case of non-specialist work on the engine. It only lasted 1000 miles after a 'professional' rebuild to 140 bhp standard

Above
Inlet valve seat standing proud of the combustion chamber

oil in it, which has literally eaten into the journal surfaces. The crankshaft journals are cut to the required size using carbide wheels, and the correct fillet radius must be observed. Many crankshafts are ruined by incompetent machinists who destroy this critical radius, making it too sharp and causing excessive stress and fractures at these points.

Polishing the journals means precisely that, using emery paper on special tongs while the crankshaft rotates. This operation is only done to clean up any light staining or scoring on journals that are within size limits.

No Lotus crankshaft must be reground more than 0.030 in. undersize. Although bearings are available beyond this limit, the risk of breakage increases alarmingly, due to the power of the engine and the extra stress imposed on the crankshaft.

Possible disasters

All the foregoing work takes us to the halfway stage of the rebuild, but before moving on to balancing, cleaning and reassembly, it is worth recapping on possible disasters that can—and do—happen. Any combustion-chamber problem, such as cracks and damage due to foreign bodies hammering up and down, has to be dealt with by welding and machining. Heavy scoring of components means they will have to be discarded or machined. Broken studs, caps etc need replacing, damaged threads will have to be helicoiled, and distorted bearing bores line-bored. Made up 'specials', masquerading as guides and seats, will have to be dealt with on a one-off basis. If the head is too far gone altogether, until new heads become available, a second-hand example will have to be found.

Normally, unless there has been crass stupidity, the engines come apart easily. Most of the problems are caused by non-professional machinists (even many respected firms seem incapable of working on Lotus twin-cam heads), who destroy perfectly good heads and crankshafts by sheer lack of knowledge. Guides are over-reamed, seats are cut at the wrong angle or over-cut into the head, or they are put in at an angle (usually to fall out later with devastating results), heads are faced at an angle so that compression increases from front to rear, blocks are rebored by too much, or are rebored with oval bores; the block face is machined at an angle, crankshafts are reground by too much, or not enough, journals

are left oval, fillet radii are destroyed. Sadly, these problems occur all too often, and many standard-block engines end up with a 0.030 in. rebore to rectify a 0.020 in. rebore, and the crankshafts have to be thrown away. I have seen just about every machining sin committed and have spent many hundreds of hours rectifying other people's mistakes.

The soundest advice is to use firms that have dealt with these engines for years, and if that is not practical because of your geographical location, use the figures in this book and give the chosen machinist a list of data so that, provided he can read, no incompetence should occur. Supply the genuine seats, guides etc yourself; do not rely on spurious parts that are made to different tolerances than those originally fitted. A machinist, for example, will not know the difference between a genuine seat and a pattern version, until he finds that the spurious one has too small or too large an outside diameter and he has to 'doctor' the head to suit. The next time around, with genuine parts, the problem will manifest itself because the correct seat will not fit! This carries on until ultimately the head has to be scrapped because of rectification machining.

The problem worsens for owners in America, Australia and European countries where very few machinists know what a Lotus twin-cam engine is. In the Elan's heyday, the Lotus dealer network was extensive throughout these three continents, and many people worked on the engines. In the late 1970s and 1980s, of course, the dealer network (outside the UK) contracted, and no one is left to understand the classic-car boom and the resurgence of the twin-cam cars. The new dealers are completely unaware that there were Lotus cars before the Esprit Turbo and Excel, so the twin-cam cars are cared for by enthusiasts and their respective owners' clubs.

Crack testing

One topic needing mention before moving on to assembly is crack testing. As this book is considering a rebuild for the road rather than for racing, unless there is a known problem this is not a normal procedure because of the extremely high cost of X-ray ultra-sound work. Heads, unless porous (very rare, in spite of being an in-phrase— see text) or cracked, never give problems. Conrods, crankshafts, blocks and camshafts can all be tested by X-rays, which will show up minute internal and external flaws. A cheaper process is

Balancing the pistons—the lightest one is placed at the rear of the scales, then the other three are balanced to it. This is achieved by removing metal from the internal diameter of the gudgeon pin

Using the second set of scales to balance the connecting rods (complete with small-end bush) end to end. Metal is removed from the eye of the small-end and the base of the big-end cap

Coupling the crankshaft to the balancer

the use of a magenta dye and powder (Ardrox process) which will only show up external cracks. However, on alloy parts, normal casting flaws, which are harmless, will also show up as cracks and have to be differentiated from the real thing.

Crack testing is vitally important for any road engine that is being tuned for racing, and most full-race engines are tested at every strip-down. Team Lotus, Ford and private engine builders, such as John Miles, laid down the strictest precautions for their race engines; every part was crack tested, and if there was any shadow of a doubt the suspect component was replaced.

It must be realized that, under normal circumstances, cracks do not just appear overnight in a road engine. They appear because of poor machining or because the component has been dropped heavily on the ground, or because someone has been stupid and placed, say, a con-rod in a vice and hit it. Very rarely is there a casting flaw which has not shown up before, or a failure due to general metal fatigue. The engine is extremely robust and, in theory, should last indefinitely because it has a cast-iron block and a good alloy head casting. On the other hand, the Coventry Climax FWE engines used in Elite models are now showing signs of stress, owing to the aluminium being over 30 years old, and with current racing programmes the engines are being caned again, resulting in head and block fractures.

Balancing and blueprinting

Balancing will improve the smoothness and longevity of the engine, by ensuring that the components are not out of balance. All crankshafts, clutches, flywheels and pistons are balanced to set tolerances, which are within the manufacturer's accepted range, but specialist firms take those limits to the extreme to create an ultra-smooth engine. It is time consuming and expensive for the manufacturer to do this, and is normally restricted to low-volume producers such as Ferrari, Porsche and Lotus who do their own balancing in-house. The benefits are always felt from the middle of the rev range upwards, and all race engines are meticulously balanced. A clutch cover, which may be 8–10 gm out and whizzing around on an 8½-in. diameter, will shake the engine and cause a vibration that can be likened to tyre imbalance at speed. Pistons are balanced weight for weight, i.e. all are matched to the lightest one and, where necessary, metal is usually removed through the gudgeon pin. Con-rods are

weighed end for end and machined to produce four identical small-end readings and four identical big-end weights. The crankshaft is balanced by drilling metal from the webs. Then the flywheel is attached and balanced to the crankshaft, again by drilling to remove metal, followed by the clutch cover which is balanced to the crankshaft and flywheel by drilling or adding heavy metal strips. Finally, the front pulley is added and balanced to the rest.

Before balancing, the pistons should be cleaned of all carbon deposits and fitted with their new rings, preferably gapped (do not forget that new pistons should be matched to the bores). The pistons should be off the con-rods, which must have their new small-end bushes fitted and new bolts in the caps for balancing. Big-end bearings are not required. The crankshaft must have its spigot bearing fitted, and the flywheel/front-pulley bolts to be used must be included. The flywheel must be true, its new ring gear fitted and all three dowels should be in place, while the clutch cover must be supplied with its bolts. The front pulley must be renewed if the flanges are chipped or broken.

The jackshaft and camshaft need not be balanced because, quite simply, their rotational mass is negligible and runs virtually about their centre-lines.

For a road engine, balancing is the best treatment that money can buy. It will prolong the life of the engine and, as a bonus, extend the rev range to a safe 7000 rpm, even though this speed is pointless because the power will be falling off and, in any case, the cut-out rotor operates at 6500, or 6750 on the Big Valve!

Blueprinting means that the engine is built to exacting standards and that all the manufacturer's fits and clearances are strictly adhered to. For a road engine, the minimum limits are used, and careful running-in is necessary. Usually for a race engine the upper limits are used, since full power will be needed almost immediately. The bottom end is all matched, i.e. pistons to bores and rods to pistons. Plastigage is used to measure bearing-to-journal clearance and, if necessary, each individual crankshaft journal is machined to match its respective bearing. The head has its combustion-chamber volumes measured using a burette and thin oil, fettling being carried out to achieve four identical readings, and the inlet and exhaust ports are balanced to each other, the aim being to achieve

Using Plasticine to act as a temporary weight

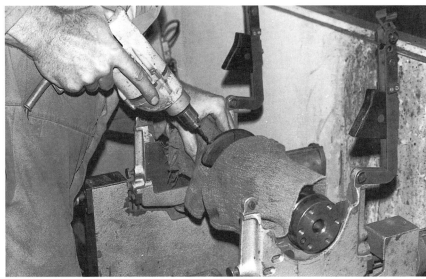

Drilling into the web to remove metal from the crankshaft

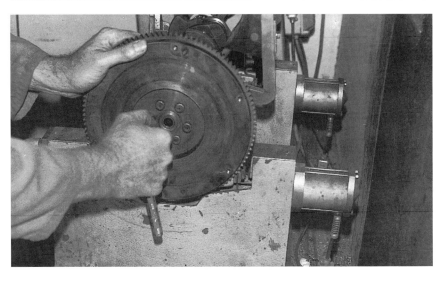

Bolting on the flywheel after the crankshaft has been brought to perfect balance. The flywheel is then balanced by drilling a series of holes along the outside edge of the face

The clutch cover is balanced to the flywheel and crankshaft

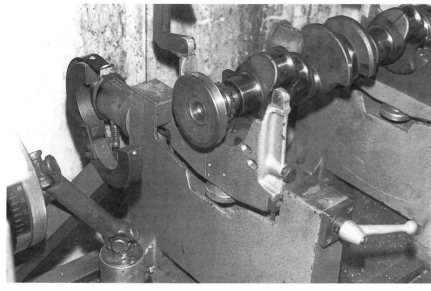

Finally, the front pulley is balanced. The entire balancing operation takes between two and three hours for one engine set

four perfectly-balanced, gas-flowed chambers.

Manufacturers do not blueprint engines from new since the work is time consuming and expensive. Indeed, for normal road engines (apart from the items already outlined, which is, in effect, a near blueprint anyway), it is not strictly necessary. A fully blueprinted engine will give approximately 3–5 bhp more towards the top end of the rpm range over the standard power curve. Blueprinting is costly, and it must be realized that for road use the expense may not be justified.

Cleaning

Before any assembly work is done, every part must be perfectly clean, otherwise one is wasting a lot of time and money in doing the rebuild. From the start, under no circumstances should any components be sand or bead blasted—so many people, who should know better, destroy engines by blasting everything in sight. It is impossible to remove all the sand or beads from the head, and eventually the hot oil will dislodge the residue which will be pumped around the engine, causing untold havoc. Most professional machine shops have degreasing tanks containing tri-chloroethylene, or some caustic solution, that will degrease parts and remove carbon and paint in one go. If the head or block has been machined, ask the machine shop for this service. It is also imperative to understand that a partially cleaned item is almost as bad as one which has not been cleaned at all; if oil sludge is disturbed, it must be removed altogether, otherwise it will circulate with the fresh oil.

For those without access to professional help, thoroughly clean everything with a water-soluble degreasant, then hose this off (preferably with a hot pressure wash). Old paint can be removed with paint stripper and a wire brush. Block sediment in the water-ways can be scraped out through the core plugs, then the waterways should be hosed out until no trace of rust or radiator or block sealants can be seen. Oilways to the main bearings and jackshaft bearings must be clear; crankshaft, jackshaft and camshaft must be spotless. All castings, such as backplate and front cover, must have no traces of gasket or sealant on them at all; all bolts and studs must have perfect threads—wire brush the threads to clean them before degreasing. Carbon deposits can be removed from the head by passing a flap wheel through the ports and carefully scraping around the combustion-chamber area. Petrol will help as a solvent, then degrease and hose off.

More time should be spent on cleaning than on anything else. It should be obvious to most people that a spotless engine will last and last, and be a joy to work on, but sadly this is not always appreciated.

When everything is gleaming, the next stage is to dry the parts thoroughly, firstly because oil and water do not mix, and secondly because in damp or very humid conditions, rust stains will appear almost within the hour. Any water remaining in the head, block, crankshaft, jackshaft or cam-shafts must be blown out with compressed air, then the parts can be left in a warm atmosphere to dry off naturally. Castings can be dried with paper towels or dry and clean cotton rags. Small items, such as sprockets, head bolts and studs, can be placed in a large tin of clean petrol, cleaned with a small (1 in.) brush and wiped dry. Make sure that the assembly area is spotless as well, and draught free so that dust is not blown over the work area.

Another important aspect that is often over-looked is the cleanliness of tools. A lot of muck is placed on bolt heads by filthy sockets, which were not cleaned after the strip-down. Wash all sockets and spanners in petrol or degreasant and wipe them dry before reassembling the engines.

If, at this stage, the rebuild has to be interrupted for any length of time, it is essential that the machined surfaces are covered with a preserving oil—the protective film will cover the surface and exclude moisture—otherwise rust will get every-where, requiring more machining to clear it. If preserving oil is unavailable, cover everything with high-melting-point grease, but not engine oil, as this will form a slurry in very damp conditions and its water content will attack the surfaces. Upon returning to the project, remove all traces of grease with petrol. If any slight staining has occurred, this can be removed by using a dry nylon pan scourer (not the wire type, as pieces of wire will break off and may cause damage), then wiping clean.

Remember that everything must be spotlessly clean and dry.

4 Engine reassembly

The use of sealants

Sealants have changed a great deal since the introduction of the Lotus twin-cam engine in 1962. Hylomar was the best and only good sealant then; it is not the best now. Do not smother everything in Hylomar, do not even use it, as it forms into hard lumps on prolonged contact with oil and eventually clogs oilways. Lotus gasket sets will have the Hylomar leaflet in them, but this probably stemmed from a job lot of leaflets printed in the 1960s! The following sealants are essential and should be used:

Graphogen—a colloidal graphite paste used on all bearing and rotating surfaces. Use it in place of oil when assembling. Oil can drain away, but Graphogen paste does not, and allows an engine to rotate even after five years of storage.

Wellseal—a non-hardening jointing compound used on gaskets (including head gasket) and core plugs.

Silicon RTV—the modern equivalent of Hylomar, red Hermetite, golden Hermetite etc. A silicon-rubber-based sealant which cures in air, giving off an acetic-acid smell. It is flexible and will move with the engine through all extremes of temperature. Use it on gaskets, D-plugs etc.

Loctite—or similar, to prevent studs and nuts coming undone.

Firegum paste—or similar, for use on exhaust-pipe joints only, and not the manifold-to-head joint.

Cylinder block

Assembly of the engine is carried out in the reverse order of dismantling, treating the block and head as two separate parts. Deal with the block first.

Fit the three core plugs in the waterways by smearing Wellseal around the edge of each plug and tapping it into place using a suitable drift (such as a socket) until the lip of the plug is flush with the block. On some blocks, all three plugs are the same size, but on others the rear plug is larger than the other two. The two on the exhaust side are always the same size. If, for any reason, the core-plug aperture in the block is damaged and there is a possibility of the plug leaking (or if it was leaking before the strip-down), fix it in place with an epoxy resin glue. Do not glue in core plugs just 'to be safe', as their purpose is to slip out easily and save the block if the water freezes solid.

Next, fit the main oil-gallery plugs and the drain plug or tap. Smear a little Wellseal around the threads and screw them in. With the block upside down, smear Graphogen (or 15-50 grade engine oil, or even EP80 gear oil) around the jackshaft bearings and install the shaft, bolting it down with its plate, new tab washer and $\frac{1}{4}$-in. UNC bolts.

Fit the new main bearings to the block and main caps (if the engine has been blueprinted, do not mix up the bearings and their respective journal positions) and smear them liberally with Graphogen or oil. Install the crankshaft, followed by the marked caps in their correct order, and nip them down. At this stage, leave off the centre main in order to check the endfloat. Add a pair of standard thrust washers by sliding each half around the journal edge into the locating groove machined in the block, pull the crankshaft back towards the rear and measure the gap between the thrust washer and crankshaft. If necessary, fit oversize thrust washers (standard 0.0025 and 0.005 in. are available); any combination may be used—one standard plus one 0.0025 in., or 0.0025 in. plus one 0.005 in.—to achieve the correct endfloat. Fit the larger size, if used singly, on the

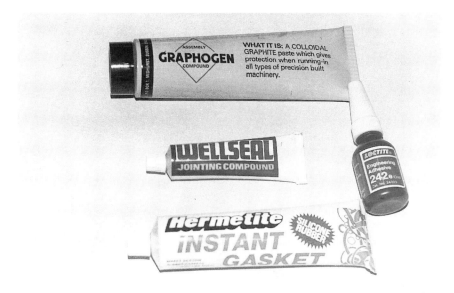

*Sealants used in rebuilding
an engine*

*Fitting the new core plugs,
using a suitable drift*

*Fit the oil-gallery plugs with
a little Wellseal sealer
around the threads*

Smearing the jackshaft bearings with Graphogen

The components making up the jackshaft assembly

Sliding in the jackshaft

Left and below left
*Tighten up the
retaining-plate bolts and
bend over the locking tab*

Placing main bearings in the cylinder block. Note that Lotus engines, compared with standard Ford units, used a superior bearing for both main and big-end positions—this was to cope with the increased horsepower produced. Lotus bearings have less tin in the bronze, and indium in the lead overlay. incidentally, the more exotic the bearing, the more expensive it is!

Smearing the bearings with Graphogen

Assembling the crankshaft

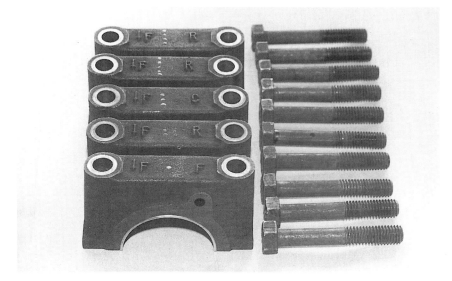

*Main caps and bolts,
showing the 1-5 markings.
The square-section caps
denote the use of a six-bolt
crankshaft; the earlier
four-bolt crank has
round-shouldered caps*

*Assembling the
main-bearing cap—also
smeared with Graphogen*

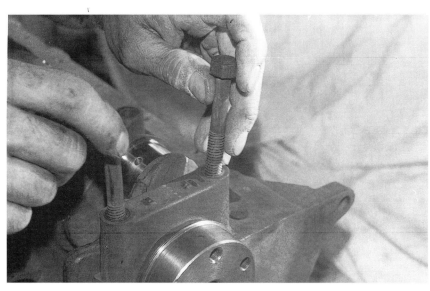

*Assembling the bearing-cap
bolts*

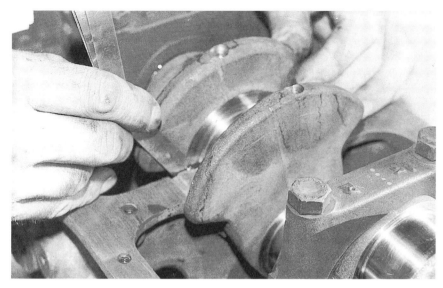

Checking thrust-washer wear, using feeler gauges

Assembling crankshaft thrust washers to the engine

Torquing the main-cap bolts in sequence—work outwards from the centre cap in three stages

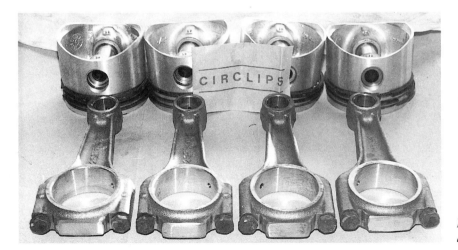

Piston and connecting-rod assemblies

Smearing the small-end bush with Graphogen. New bushes must be reamed to fit the gudgeon pin

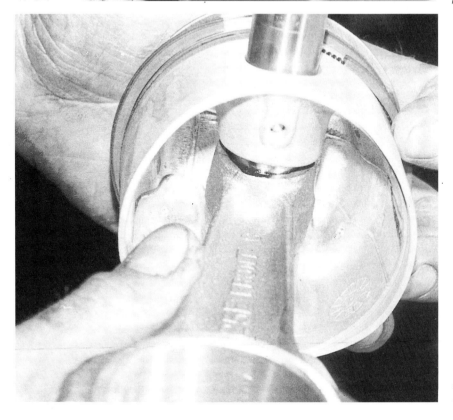

Sliding the gudgeon pin through the small-end bush

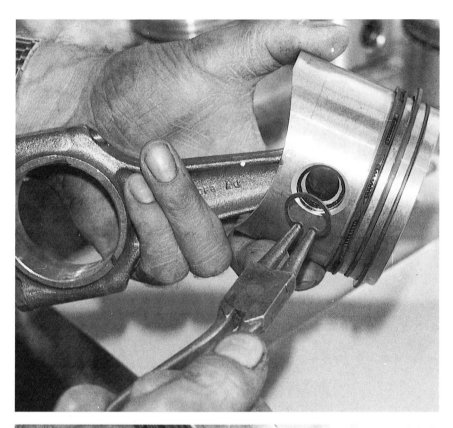

Fitting the small-end circlip

Checking piston-ring gaps in the bores. Note the fresh hone marks

clutch (rear) side of the centre main. Smear Graphogen on the thrust faces and position the washers with the oil cut-outs facing outwards (i.e. towards the crank face—the plain side abuts the centre main). Locate the centre main cap and torque down the bolts in three stages (20, 40 and 60 lb ft), working from the centre outwards. Make sure the crankshaft turns freely at each stage. There is no need to put Loctite on the bolt threads.

Assemble the pistons to their respective connecting rods by smearing Graphogen or oil around the small-end bush and pushing the gudgeon pin through, fit the circlips at each end. Make sure the front of the piston matches the front of the rod, otherwise the valve cut-outs will be in the wrong place. The gudgeon pins are a sliding fit, but if they are slightly tight, warm the pistons by using a fan or radiant heater, or by placing them in hot water to expand the aluminium.

Support the block in its normal position and gap the piston rings by pushing each one in turn about $\frac{1}{2}$ in. down its respective bore with the top of a piston and measure the gap with a feeler gauge. If it is too tight, file it to the correct gap—do not leave any sharp burrs. If the gap is too wide, there has been an error in machining the bore, or the wrong rings have been obtained. Normally, all ring sets are perfectly matched and not many builders even bother with this operation, but it should always be done. Then carefully fit the rings to the pistons from the top, opening each out and sliding it down into the correct groove; the oil control ring is first, followed by the number two compression ring, and finally the number one compression ring.

Fit the big-end bearings to the con-rods and their caps, smearing the bearing surface with Graphogen. Smother the piston and rings with Graphogen or oil, and smear the bores as well. Then use a piston clamp to fit the piston assemblies in their respective bores. Tap each piston down gently; if definite resistance is felt, undo the clamp and start again—do not keep on hammering, as a ring may break, causing much heartache later on. With all four pistons in place, turn the block over and locate the bearing caps. Nip them up with new bolts and make sure the crank rotates freely. Then torque down in two stages, first to 25 and finally 45 lb ft. Again, there is no need to Loctite the threads.

The oil pipes are tapped in place by putting a bolt in the end of each tube and hitting the bolt head gently. The strainer is then placed on the large tube by its guide, and the tabs bent over to retain it (six-bolt type). The earlier four-bolt oil-strainer pipe slides in and locks up with the nut and olive.

The front cover should be assembled next. Preheat the cover, either with a heater or by placing it in boiling water for five minutes, press in the water-pump bearing and fit the locating wire clip. Do not hit the bearing shaft as failure will result, press only on the outside casing with a suitable drift (such as a socket). Press on the hub flange until it is flush with the bearing shaft, using a vice or press and making sure that the hub is fitted squarely and the right way round. Smear a little RTV silicon around the seal and press it into its location in the housing. Make sure the $\frac{1}{8}$-in. drain hole is perfectly clear, then smear a little RTV silicon around the bottom O-ring on the alloy ring and locate it in the housing. Press well in, then fit the impellor seal the correct way round, carbon face to carbon face (plain face to plain face). Finally, press on the impellor to give 0.025–0.030 in. clearance between the vanes and the housing.

NOTE The foregoing applies to the new and revised Lotus water pump, introduced from 1985, which does away with the brass slinger. If any old types are left, the procedure is the same, except that the slinger is drifted down the shaft first to $\frac{1}{8}$ in. off the bearing itself. Then the bearing is pressed in as before.

The new type impellor seal is very tight to push down over the bearing shaft, so do not worry, for resistance is perfectly normal. It must be emphasized that the water pump is very easy to fit, but people sometimes panic. However, the front cover must be in good order; if the casting has corroded away, no pump on earth will seal.

If the casing is still warm, the oil seal can be pushed in—smear a little Wellseal around the periphery—or it can be pressed in. Fit a new timing-chain damper and put some Loctite on the $\frac{1}{4}$ in. UNC screw threads. Make sure the screws are tight, otherwise if one falls out, devastation could result! If a new front cover is used, the dipstick tube must be drifted in to match its original position exactly. Failure to do so will result in a false oil-level reading always being given on the dipstick. This simple oversight causes more oil problems than is necessary, since people may think they have a full sump when only

Fitting piston assemblies into the bores, using a piston clamp, and gently tapping down with a light hammer handle. The pistons have also been smeared with Graphogen

Fitting the big-end cap, the bearing being smeared with Graphogen

Torquing the big-end bolts

Six-bolt engine oil-strainer and pick-up pipe assemblies

Tapping in the drain tube with a light engineer's hammer, using a bolt to support the tube

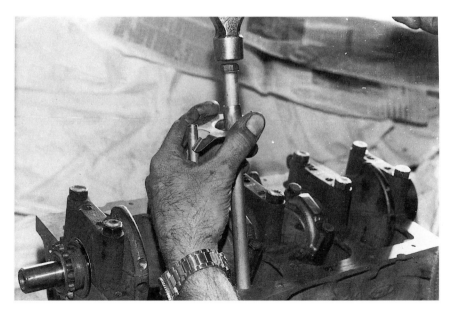

The strainer tube being fitted, also using a bolt as a support

Bending over the oil-strainer retaining tags

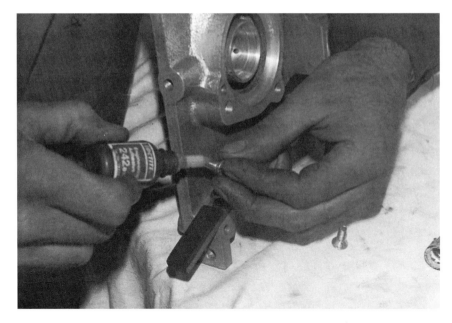

Fitting the timing-chain damper. Remember to place a little Loctite on the screw threads

The water-pump seal bleed hole must be completely clear, and the seal area must be free of corrosion

Genuine Lotus water-pump components

Fitting the water-pump bearing, using a press. Before doing this, heat the cover to around 90 degrees Celsius

Fitting the bearing retaining clip

Installing the hub flange, once again using a press

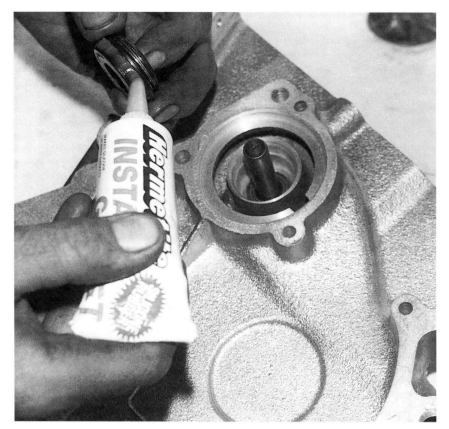

Smearing a little silicon RTV around the base of the seal before locating it in the cover

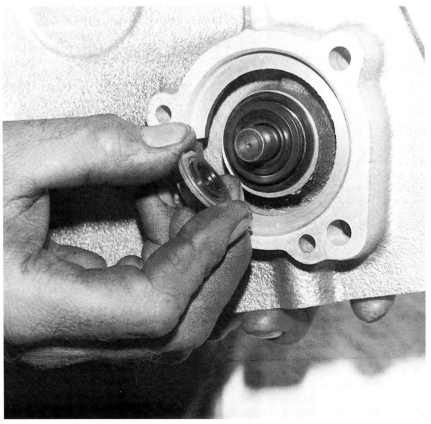

Fitting the water-pump impellor seal

Fitting the impellor housing, using a little RTV around the bottom locating O-ring. Note the locating lug

Pressing on the impellor, using a feeler gauge to measure the running clearance

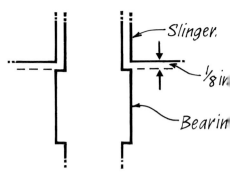

Above
Water-pump slinger-to-bearing clearance (not fitted in post-1985 kits)

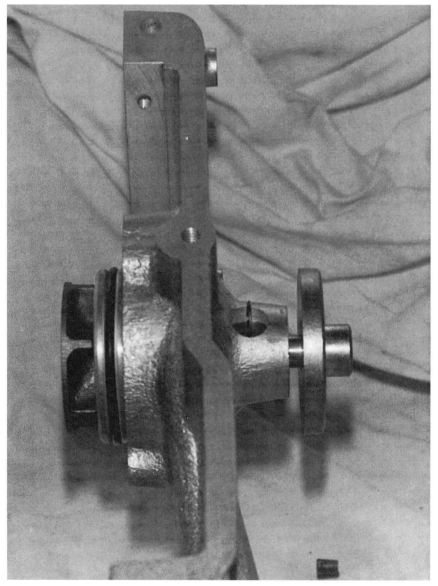

A fully-assembled water pump

Pressing in the front-cover oil seal, with a little Wellseal applied around the outside

Using a drift to tap the dipstick tube into a pre-warmed front cover. It is essential to insert the tube to the correct depth

Locating the backplate with its bolt. Both sides of the gasket have been treated with Wellseal

Fitting the jackshaft sprocket with its lock tabs and oil slinger

4 pints (2 litres) are actually in it. This gives rise to no oil pressure on very cold mornings, when the oil cannot drain back quickly enough into the sump upon start up, or oil 'surge' on bends, with no oil pressure when hot.

With the front cover fully assembled, the back-plate is fitted next—smear both sides of its gasket with Wellseal and place it on the block. Locate the backplate with several of the front-cover bolts and torque the $\frac{1}{4}$ in. UNC backplate retaining bolt with its spring washer to 6–8 lb ft. Withdraw the front-cover bolts. Fit the crankshaft oil slinger and the jackshaft sprocket, together with a new lock tab. Torque to 15 lb ft and bend over the tabs. Install a new chain, smear a little RTV around the second O-ring on the water-pump impellor housing, around the pump moulding boss itself and down both side mating faces (note that there is no gasket here), and fit into the backplate. Bolt up the assembly, using the $\frac{1}{4}$ in. UNC bolts, $\frac{5}{16}$ in. UNC bolt and $\frac{1}{4}$ in. UNF bolt and Nylocs. Torque all $\frac{1}{4}$ in. bolts to 7 lb ft, and the $\frac{5}{16}$ in. bolt to 12 lb ft. Wipe away any excess sealant that has oozed out.

On the six-bolt crankshaft, fit the rear oil seal into its housing by placing the casting in hot water for a few minutes, smearing a little Wellseal around the seal's periphery and pressing it in with your fingers. Always check that the wire ring is joined tightly, pull it out and tug the join—if it is loose, twist it to tighten it, and fit back over the rubber lip. Smear Wellseal on both sides of the gasket and place it on the housing, smear a little grease around the lip of the oil seal and slide it over the crankshaft. Then torque the four $\frac{5}{16}$ in. UNC bolts and spring washers to 18 lb ft. With the four-bolt crankshaft, place the asbestos-rope seal in its housing, smear Wellseal on both sides of the gasket, place it on the housing, wipe a little engine oil over the seal-to-crank face, and bolt the housing to the block.

Run a bead of RTV along the block face and fit the sump gaskets. Then install the cork sealing blocks on the front cover and rear oil seal (six-bolt) and tap them gently into place. Make sure they are fully home—it may be necessary to trim off a tiny piece—and lay another bead of RTV along the gaskets and over the corks, paying particular attention to the 'corners' where the gaskets meet the corks. Offer up the sump and push it down gently over the corks, bolting it up using the $\frac{1}{4}$ in. UNC setscrews and washers. Progressively torque it down to 8 lb ft. This

operation may need repeating three or four times before the gaskets and cork are fully compressed. Wipe away any excess sealant.

On the four-bolt-crankshaft engine, smear a little RTV around the sump's rear cut-out and fit the other half of the asbestos-rope seal. Position the gaskets on RTV, smear oil over the seal and fit the sump, taking care not to dislodge the seal in the sump, otherwise a massive and immediate oil leak will occur. Place a new copper or nylon washer on the sump drain plug and torque it to 25 lb ft.

If the spigot bearing has not been fitted already (i.e. for balancing), fit it now, using a suitable drift to drive it in up to its location. Make sure it is the right way round with its 'oil seal' lip at the rear. Install the flywheel, making sure that the mating faces are clean and that the balance marks (if any) line up. Loctite the threads and torque the bolts, in two stages, to 45 lb ft. On the four-bolt engine, renew the lock tab and bend the tabs over after torquing up.

Fit the clutch, using a clutch alignment tool, and make sure that the plate is positioned correctly (it is marked 'flywheel side'). Torque the clutch cover to 20 lb ft. Make sure that all balance marks are aligned correctly, otherwise the clutch will vibrate at speed. Repaint or re-scribe the balance marks if necessary. This is essential, in case, at any time in the future, the engine has to be stripped again.

Slide on the front pulley and rotate the engine so that the pistons are half-way down the bores. The block assembly is now complete, but less oil and fuel pumps and the distributor, which are put on later.

Cylinder head

If necessary, fit new core plugs to die-cast and early sand-cast heads, or the brass plugs to late sand-cast heads, installing them with Wellseal. This is not a normal operation, so only do it if the plugs are weeping.

Next, lap in the valves with a valve grinding (sucker) tool, in the usual manner, placing a little fine grinding paste around the valve face and smearing thin oil around the valve stem. Lap each valve in turn until an even, light-grey ring appears on the seats. Wipe off all traces of grinding paste and apply a little engineer's blue to the valve face. Refit the valve and give it one even turn. Lift it out, and if an even ring of the same intensity blue is seen, the seat is perfect. If the blue appears heavier

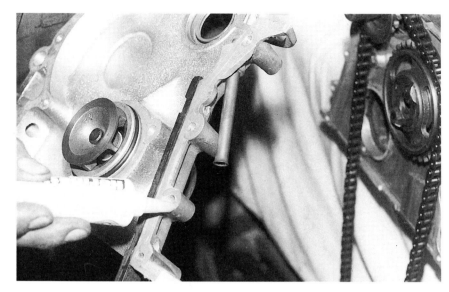

Lock tabs bent over and the chain fitted. Place a bead of RTV on the front-cover mating face—this does not have a gasket

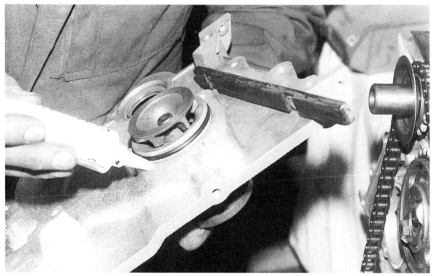

Running a bead of RTV around the top locating O-ring and around the water-pump-boss mating face

Gently press on the front cover and torque it down

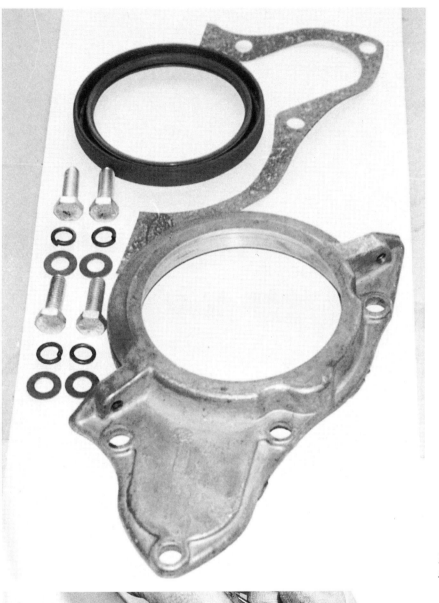

*Rear oil-seal components—
six-bolt crank*

*Checking that the wire
retaining ring is secure on
the seal*

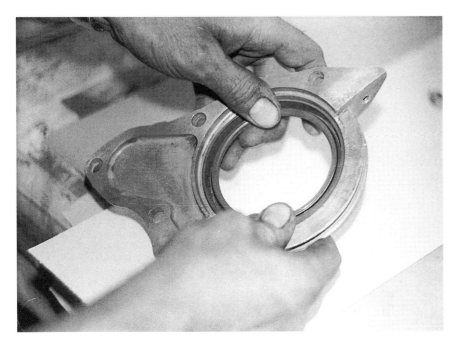

Pressing in the rear oil seal, using one's thumbs, after pre-warming the alloy housing. A thin smear of Wellseal around the edge of the seal helps

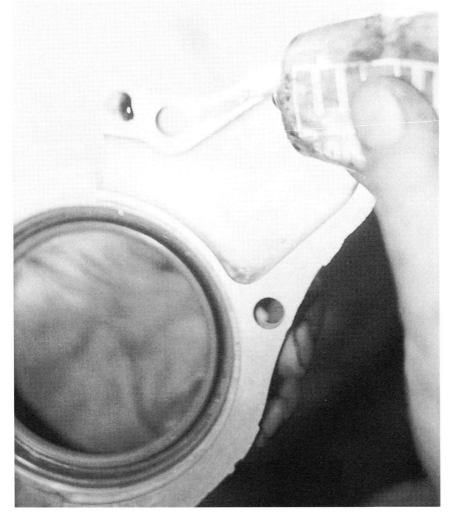

Smear Wellseal on the housing

Smear Wellseal on the gasket

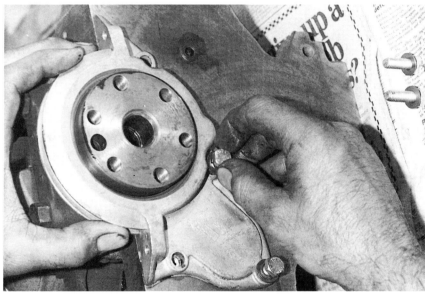

Gently ease the seal over the crankshaft—with a smear of grease around the lip—and bolt it up

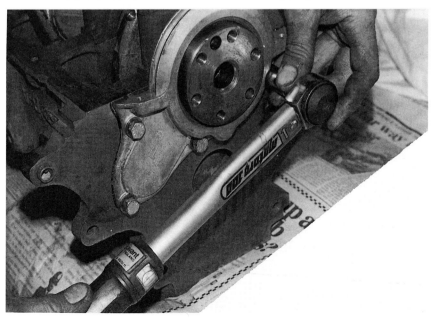

Torquing the rear seal housing

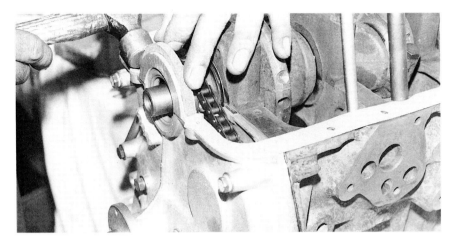

Fitting the sump-pan gaskets and the front-cover cork seal, tapping the latter gently into place to ensure that it is well down. RTV is used on the block surface

Placing a bead of RTV on the sump side of the gasket and cork seals, making sure that some gets well into the corners

Fitting the sump

An early four-bolt sump pan, showing the smaller rear cut-away where the rope or cork seal locates. Note, also, the two rear channelled bolt guides

Driving in the spigot bearing, using a suitable drift (this applies to all Elans, four-speed +2s, Lotus-Cortinas and Escorts)

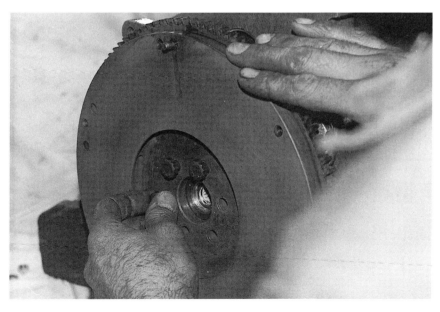

Fitting the flywheel to a six-bolt crank. A new starter ring gear has already been fitted

Locating the clutch plate, using the clutch centralizing tool

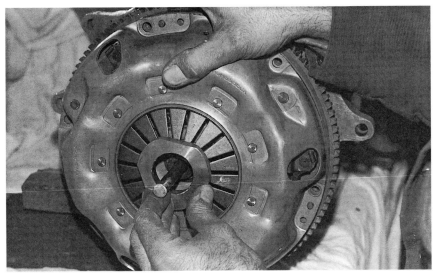

Fit the clutch cover on its dowels and bolt it up. All balance marks must be aligned

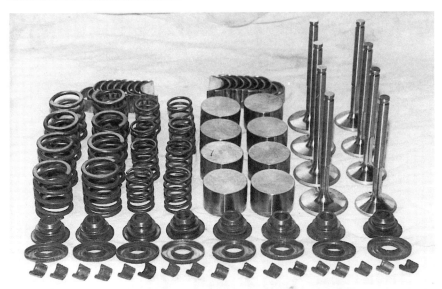

Valve-gear components

Lapping in the valves, using engineer's blue to achieve a perfect seat. Note the complete evenness of the number two and three inlet seats. Only fine grinding paste is used. Do not use a coarse paste

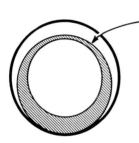

Bad lapping-in area of poor seating that will give rise to problems later on.

A complete, uniform ring of colour will indicate that the valves and seats are lapped correctly

Inserting valves, using Graphogen on the stems. Note the evenness of the seats. This head has been fly cut to true it up

on one side than the other, continue lapping in until an even colour is seen. It is essential to achieve a good, even seat, otherwise compression may be lost and, in time, valve burning may occur on the exhaust side.

When all the valves have been lapped, number them from one to four, inlet or exhaust, and thoroughly clean off all traces of paste on the head and valve faces; do not leave any grit in the ports. Make sure that the guides are completely clean. Assemble each valve in the head by smearing Graphogen on to the valve stem and fitting the valve spring seat, the inner and outer valve springs, and the top spring retainer, pushing the assembly down with the special valve-spring compressor. Fit the two collets and lift off the compressor. When all are installed, support the head off the valves and lightly tap each valve spring retainer, using a suitable drift (such as a plug socket), to settle the collets. Make sure that there are no burrs on the collets to prevent the retainer seating properly, as this will lead to false tappet-clearance readings later on.

Fit any new head, camshaft-cap, exhaust or inlet stud by Loctiting the threads and winding it in with two locked nuts or a stud extractor. Locate the camshaft bearings in the head and in the caps, and smear them with Graphogen. Note that the four 'half' shells go at the rear on numbers one and ten caps. Insert a nominal set of tappet shims (the original shims will be useless with new seats, valves etc, or if existing seats have been refaced) and apply Graphogen around the tappets (before placing them in the head. Do not mix up the tappets if they have been matched to the new machined sleeves; keep them in their correct order.

Lay the camshafts in their respective banks (do not forget to replace the end plugs, otherwise there will be no oil pressure) and torque down the caps to 9 lb ft. Make sure that each camshaft turns freely and that the cap numbers are adjacent to the numbers stamped on the head. A common mistake is to confuse caps six and nine. If the camshaft binds up, release each cap in turn to find which one is causing the problem. Make sure that its dowel is not oval and thus causing distortion, and that the bearing is seating correctly. If all appears to be in order, yet the camshaft still binds, a line-boring operation is the only answer (see earlier). Do not continue, because as soon as the engine turns over, the camshaft bearing will be wrecked, so will the camshaft, and the drive chain

will receive increased loads. (NOTE There are no 'genuine' oversize camshaft bearings.) Fit the respective camshaft sprockets with their special stepped washers and half-head bolts. The exhaust sprocket has 'EX' etched on it. Do not mix them up.

Valve clearances

Turn the inlet camshaft by using a $\frac{5}{8}$ in. socket on the sprocket bolt so that number one lobe points upwards, i.e. the heel of the camshaft is directly above the tappet, and measure the clearance between the heel and the top of the tappet. Check all the inlet-valve clearances in this way, and note down each feeler-gauge reading. Repeat the procedure for the exhaust-side cam. For all engines, inlet clearances should be 0.005–0.007 in., and exhaust clearances 0.009–0.011 in. If you are rebuilding an engine with the original exhaust valves still fitted (this applies to engines before number 9952), use an exhaust-valve clearance of 0.006–0.008 in.

Having measured all the clearances, the next step is to calculate the shim size needed to obtain the correct clearances. For example, suppose there is a nominal 0.090 in. shim fitted to number one inlet, and the clearance measured is 0.030 in. The total is 0.120 in., less the required clearance of 0.006 in. (mid-way between 0.005 and 0.007 in.), giving a required shim size of 0.114 in. Alternatively, suppose there is a nominal 0.090 in. shim fitted to number one exhaust, and the clearance measured is 0.002 in. The total is 0.092 in., minus the required clearance of 0.010 in. (mid-way between 0.009 and 0.011 in.), making the actual shim required a 0.082 in. size.

When measuring the clearance, be careful not to cant the shim which would provide a false reading. Be wary of, say, nominal 0.090 in. shims giving 0.020 in. clearances, yet the fourth one measured not giving any clearance at all, or a very large clearance. In this situation, something is not seating properly (there may be burrs on the collet holding down the retainer and valve to give a larger gap), or the shim is canted, providing no gap at all, or the machinist who fitted the valve seat, or refaced it, has made a mistake and not told anyone!

With all the clearances worked out, remove the inlet camshaft and the tappets, using a valve sucker, and replace the nominal shims with those of the correct size. Repeat this procedure for the exhaust side. Then torque the cam caps to 9 lb ft

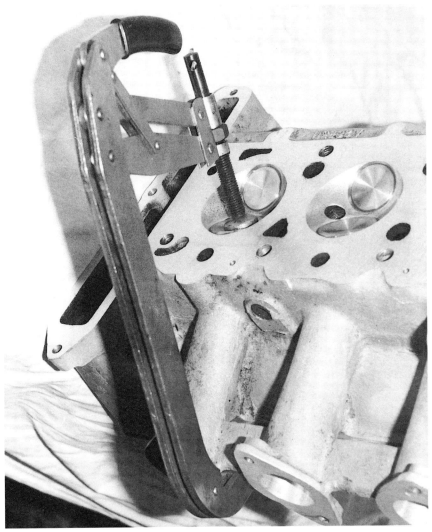

Using the correct
'deep-throat' valve-spring
compressor

Assembling the valve
collets, using long-nosed
pliers

Fitting new camshaft-cap studs, using a reversible stud-extractor tool

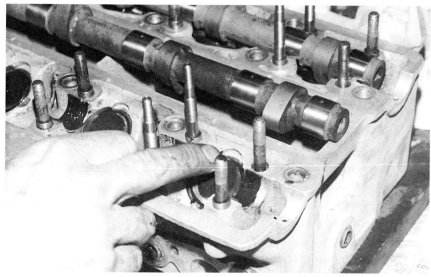

Smear Graphogen on the cam shells and tappets

Assembling the camshafts

*Checking valve clearances.
Note the use of plain nuts
to facilitate removal and
replacement of the camshaft
while adjusting the
clearances. Nyloc nuts lose
their effectiveness if
repeatedly tightened and
unscrewed; they should be
used only once*

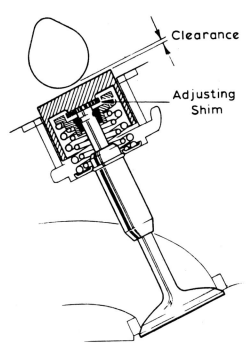

*Measure valve clearance
between the heel of the cam
and the top of the tappet*

again, and recheck the clearances. If they fall within limits, leave well alone—they will have to be checked again when running in. However, you may find that you have to repeat the operation—I am sorry, but it is very important to get these settings absolutely right.

When dealing with the odd one- or two-thou discrepancy, remember: to INCREASE the clearance, DECREASE the shim thickness; to DECREASE the clearance, INCREASE the shim thickness.

With all the valve clearances correctly adjusted, the cylinder head is virtually ready for mating to the block. Fit a new grommet for the breather pipe—make sure it goes in evenly—or fit the elbow for the earlier pipe (this was used on engines built until early 1968). Install a new thermostat (either with 88 degrees Celsius or 78 degrees Celsius setting), making sure that the bleed hole points towards the radiator; apply Wellseal on both sides of the gasket and torque down the two $\frac{5}{16}$ in. UNC bolts to 15 lb ft. Add the timing-chain sprocket. If you are renewing the sprocket and/or carrier, fit the bushed bolt with Loctite on its thread, and torque to 40–45 lb ft. Then dot-punch it in three places to press brass into the bolt, preventing it becoming loose. Smear Graphogen around the bush first. Fit a new crush washer on to the pivot bolt, Graphogen the spindle, and Loctite the thread, then insert the bolt through the head and carrier, torquing it to 40–45 lb ft. The use of the Lotus washer is important—the wrong type (i.e. an ordinary fibre washer) will lead to loosening of the bolt and, in extreme cases, the pin will fall out, causing untold damage. The head is now ready to be fitted.

Assembling the head to the block
Make sure the block face is still spotless, then fit two modified head studs (saw off the bolt head and cut a screwdriver slot in the top) at the right-hand front corner and left-hand rear to act as location guides. These must be used to locate the gasket, otherwise damage may result due to the head and gasket sliding around. Apply RTV to both sides of the cork front-cover gasket and place it on the front cover, then smear RTV around both ends of the new head-to-block rubber and place it in the block. Coat both sides of the head gasket with a thin, even coat of Wellseal and locate it on the block (if Wellseal is not available, fit it dry; do not use any other jointing compound) and then fit the head, making sure that there are

no traces of oil on the face. Check that the head-to-block rubber is located properly, otherwise oil leakage will occur. Fit the head studs (any old thin-shouldered studs must be discarded and new ones used) and their special washers (only these washers must be used—the normal type will dig into the head under load and give a false torque reading). The D-washers go on left-hand front (inlet) and left-hand rear (inlet) to give the necessary clearance for the camshaft and number one bearing cap. Torque down the head in three stages (25, 45 and 65 lb ft). The sequence is shown on page 145.

The $\frac{5}{16}$ in. UNC timing-cover bolts are torqued to 15 lb ft, and the sequence is also shown on page 145. Torque the head bolts again and do the front cover three times to make sure that the cork gasket is compressed fully. Wipe away any excess sealant.

The next stage is the valve timing, and the following procedure is a continuation of the normal rebuild, whereby the timing chain is set up correctly over the sprockets. If different camshafts have been fitted, the following section details how to set the valve timing from scratch.

If the engine was running correctly before the rebuild and all is relatively standard, the camshafts remain the same and have not been reprofiled, and the head has not been skimmed excessively, make sure both camshafts are rocking on number four cylinder, in which case the camshaft sprocket marks will be in line at the front. Rotate the crankshaft until the notch on the pulley lines up with the TDC mark on the front cover. Undo both camshaft sprockets and remove them. Pull up the timing chain with a length of bent wire, or long, thin-nosed pliers, and loop it over both camshafts—making sure the chain has not snagged on the other two sprockets. First fit the exhaust sprocket over the chain and bolt it to the camshaft, then fit the inlet sprocket in the same way. Smear Graphogen over the timing-chain plunger and insert it into the front cover, followed by the spring and the retaining bolt. Apply Loctite to the coarse thread (not the fine UNF tensioner thread) and, with a new Lotus crush washer, torque down to 40 lb ft. Screw in the tensioner thread until resistance is felt, and keep going until the total chain movement across the top run is $\frac{1}{2}$ in. (13 mm). Then nip up the $\frac{5}{16}$ in. UNF Nyloc and slowly rotate the engine through a complete revolution—all the marks should line up correctly as shown on page 147.

Torquing down the caps with new Nyloc nuts after the correct valve clearances have been established

The head ready to mate with the block. Note that plain nuts are still on number one cap, because this will need removing to allow the socket to fit over the rear head stud

Keep the head like this, to prevent damage to the valve faces after the camshafts have been fitted

The block assembly, ready to accept the head

Fitting the oil drain tube that links the head to the block. RTV is used around both 'threads'

Modify two head bolts to act as guides for fitting the head and gasket. Use Wellseal on both sides of the latter

Use RTV on both faces of the front-cover gasket

Sliding the head down over the studs to mate with the block

The head studs and their special washers are in place, and the locating stud is being removed

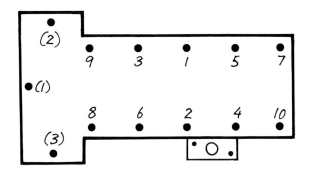

Cylinder-head-bolt tightening sequence. Figures in brackets refer to timing-cover bolt sequence

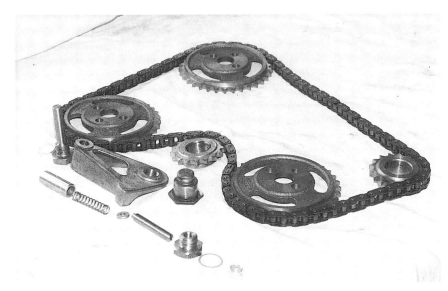

The complete timing-chain gear and tensioner assemblies

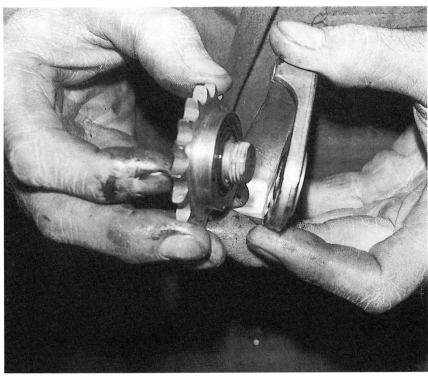

Fitting a new timing-chain sprocket to its brass carrier

The carrier being positioned with the aid of long-nosed pliers. Note the special washer on the pin

The new tensioner thread being peened over its washer

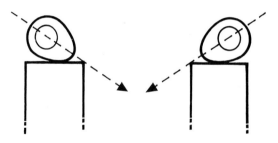

When setting the valve timing, make sure both camshafts are rocking on number four cylinder

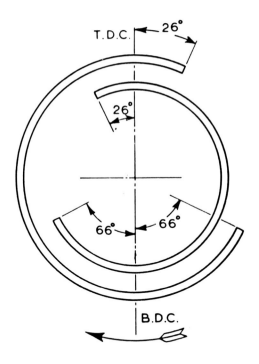

Left
This is the typical valve timing of the engine

Below
Note the location of timing marks on the front cover of the twin-cam engine, also the correct chain tension

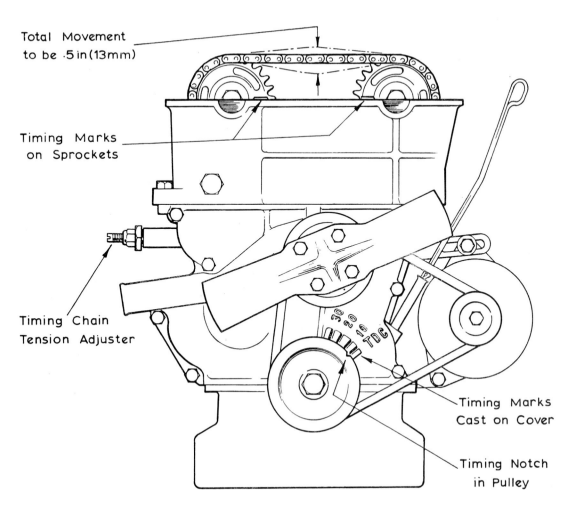

Pulling up the chain over the exhaust-camshaft sprocket

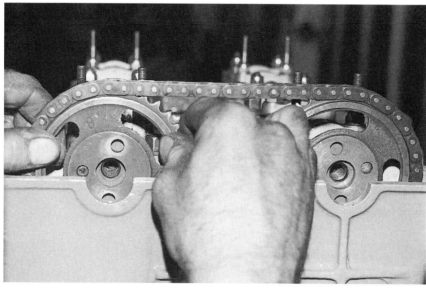

Fitting the inlet sprocket

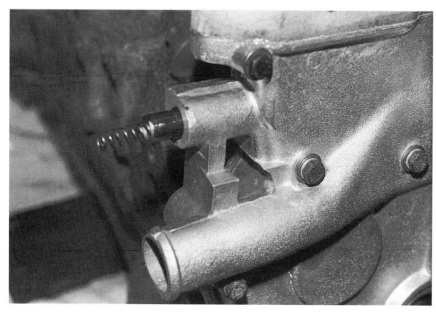

Plunger and spring lubricated with Graphogen

Fitting the tensioner thread. Note the special washer. Loctite the coarse thread. The front hub pulley has already been assembled

Adjusting the chain tension

Painting the engine Lotus grey

Screwing in the inlet and exhaust studs, using a reversible stud extractor; apply Loctite to the threads

Fitting the new breather grommet and any unions in the head. The D-plug is sitting on a bead of RTV

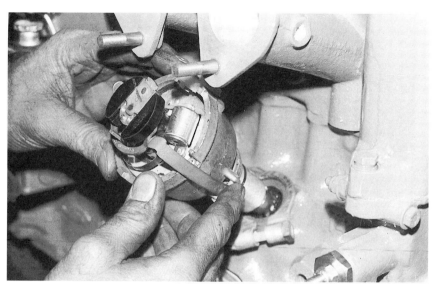

Fitting the distributor. Note the correct type of cut-out rotor arm

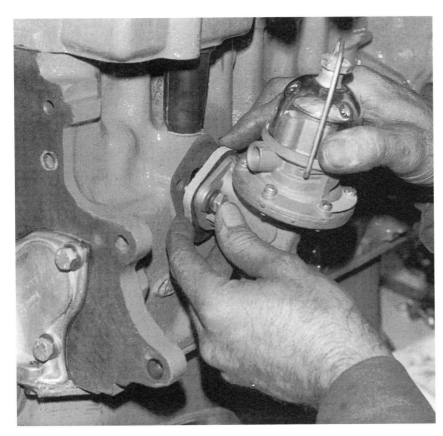

Fitting the fuel pump, with its packing piece smeared with Wellseal on both sides

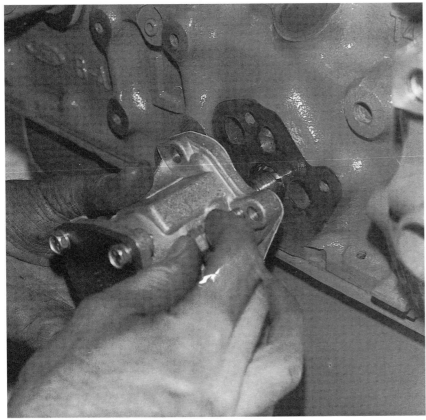

Fitting the new oil pump, having first primed the gears with oil. Wellseal is smeared on both sides of the gasket

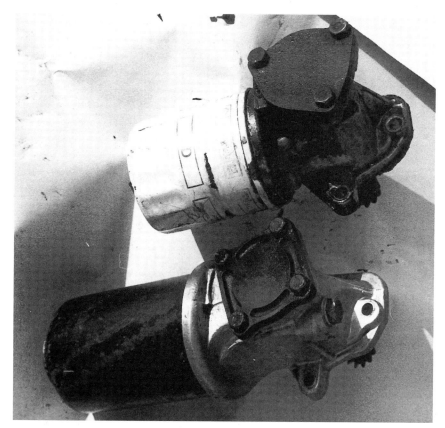

*Early and late oil filters—
screw-on canister and
separate element types*

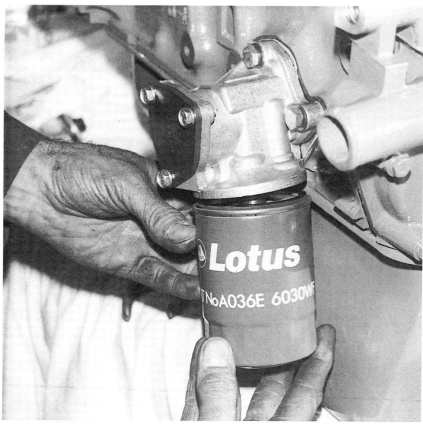

*Fitting the Lotus oil filter,
which is longer than the
usual Mini type*

*The cam gasket being
assembled. Use Wellseal, or
RTV, on both sides*

Fitting the cam cover

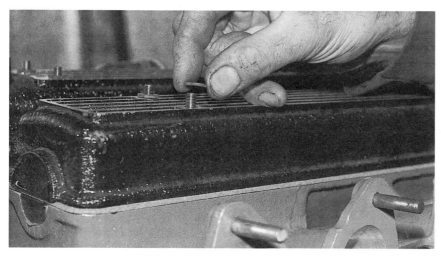

*Fitting the Senloc washers
before torquing down*

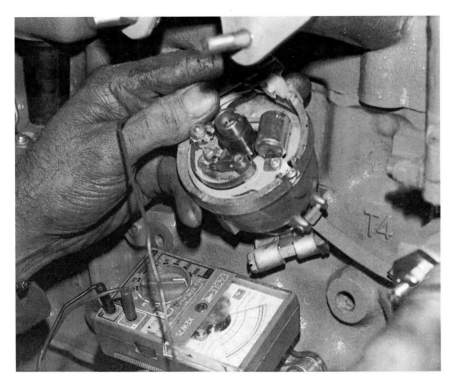

Adjusting the opening of the distributor points, using a multi-meter. The front-pulley timing marks will be on a correct static setting—10 degrees BTDC

A Lotus Elan Big Valve engine, complete and awaiting collection. Note the correct use of alloy spacer plates for fixing the Weber carburettors. The plastic type of O-rings should not be used, because they deteriorate through exposure to heat and fuel. The HT leads are routed up through the inlet manifold, as was normal from 1971 onwards

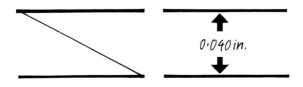

0.040 in.

Correct gap between spring coils of Thackery washers

If all is correct, finalize the chain tension by rotating the engine a few more times and then tighten up the lock nut. If incorrect, slacken the tension, undo the inlet-camshaft sprocket and move it round by one or more teeth in the correct direction. Then, with a pair of locking grips, carefully grasp the inlet camshaft and turn it slightly so the sprocket can be attached to it again. Adjust the tension and rotate the engine once more to check that all is now correct. Remember that the fixed run of chain from crankshaft to exhaust sprocket must always be tight, and that the cam lobes on number four cylinder must always point in towards each other by an equal amount. Note that very few engines left Lotus with the camshaft-sprocket marks spot on. Do not worry if the marks appear to be slightly out, one up, one down—this is normal.

Torque the camshaft-sprocket bolts and the front-pulley bolt to 25 lb ft. Apply a bead of RTV around the cam D-plugs and fit them in place. Use either Wellseal or RTV on both sides of the cam-cover gasket, fit it in place and attach the cam cover with new plain, Senloc and $\frac{1}{4}$ in. UNF Nyloc nuts. Torque down to 6 lb ft. Do this three times and wipe away excess sealant.

At this stage, if the engine is to be painted, paint it grey. No engine ever left the factory in any colour other than Lotus grey. An air-drying enamel is ideal, and one coat is sufficient.

When the paint is dry, fit the fuel pump and the oil pump (use Wellseal on both sides of the gaskets and torque the $\frac{5}{16}$ in. UNC bolts to 15 lb ft). With the mechanical fuel pump do not forget the packing block, and that the lever arm sits on top of the jackshaft lobe—failure to observe either of these points will result in serious damage. As a precaution, the oil pump should always be renewed (see later) to safeguard the rebuilt engine. Before fitting it, prime the gears with a little engine oil, screw on the oil filter or

place a new element in the bowl and bolt it up. Add the dynamo/alternator brackets and water-pump hub/fan assembly, tightening the four $\frac{1}{4}$-in. UNC bolts to 8 lb ft. Next, install the distributor and set the ignition timing. Position the crankshaft at 10 degrees BTDC and engage the distributor with the helical gear so that the rotor arm points to the number one contact. Connect a test bulb or meter and rotate the distributor body until the contact points just begin to open, i.e. the light goes out or the meter reading returns to zero. Clamp up the body and fit the cut-out rotor.

NOTE All engines had a 6500 rpm cut-out, except for the Big Valve engines which had a 6750 rpm setting. The cut-out is there for a purpose—it protects the engine from over-revving—and there is no advantage in removing it, as the power curve is already falling off quickly at these high engine speeds.

Fit the spark plugs and torque them to 20 lb ft. Then undo them and tighten again to 25 lb ft. Fit the distributor cap and leads to the plugs, the firing order being 1-3-4-2.

Finally, if the carburettors are Webers or Dellortos, renew the O-rings on the alloy spacer plates (do not use the plastic integral O-ring type, as after a time the plastic hardens and becomes brittle due to attack from heat and fuel—they are not suitable for twin-cam, if any, engine applications). Fit new Thackery washers and tighten up so that the gap between the spring coils is approximately 0.040 in.—the carburettors are supposed to be flexibly mounted.

The same applies to all Strombergs—renew the adaptor block gaskets and the balance-pipe O-rings, the carburettor/adaptor-block O-rings and the Thackery washers. With American emission engines, install the cross-over pipes after the engine is in place.

Fit the engine mountings and/or brackets, if required, and the engine is ready to run.

5 Valve timing

An engine's valve timing is governed by the camshaft, the design of which dictates the opening and closing of the valves. This, in turn, governs the whole cycle of induction and exhaust. Correct valve timing is critically important to the operation of any engine, and if it is incorrect it upsets the entire firing cycle. As applied to the twin-cam, if the timing is out of adjustment by one or two teeth, the firing cycle will be out of phase, and performance will drop away considerably.

When the head has been skimmed it sits lower in relation to the block, placing the camshafts lower too. If a lot of metal has been removed from the head, so that the chain tension has to be wound right in to compensate, valve timing is seriously altered, with the possibility of valves (the inlet, usually) touching the pistons. Finally, with a 'performance' camshaft fitted, or a reprofiled original, the valve timing will also be different. By bolting on a special camshaft, but not altering the valve timing and valve clearances to suit, the promised 'instant' performance gain will be severely reduced. Many twin-cam engines are made virtually undriveable by the use of supposedly '160 bhp' camshafts that have not been timed in any way.

Camshaft design is an exact science, and a complete book could be written on this subject alone, but it must be clearly understood that the correct valve clearances must be maintained, otherwise damage can occur to the valve gear. If valve clearances are too large, the high accelerations imparted to the valve gear can cause excessive wear, noise, valve-seat hammering and reduced valve-gear component life. With too little clearance, exhaust valves can burn out, the engine becoming 'fluffy' and inflexible at low running speeds. Both conditions adversely affect the power and torque developed by the engine.

Accordingly, each cam lobe has a designed 'lead-in' time. Lobes vary—in general, a short valve opening time may be accompanied by a peaky lobe, while a longer opening time may be accompanied by a broad lobe. On reprofiled camshafts, the base circle will be reduced in diameter, necessitating a thicker shim to achieve the same valve clearance.

With different specifications of camshaft, the valve clearance may differ from the standard setting. It must be realized that the clearances are designed to meet the camshaft's requirements at normal running temperature; when cold, the valve clearance is not the same as when hot, due to the different expansion rates existing in valve stems and associated components. Different valve materials will expand at different rates, hence there is a wider clearance on the exhaust side. With all camshafts, the setting is arranged to give the optimum hot clearance at or around the middle point on the ramp. These clearances will vary from camshaft to camshaft because of the lobe profile and different valve/component material specifications. These points are not normally understood by firms which offer 'instant' performance. A BRM Phase IV profile may now run in a different way than it used to do when BRM made it in 1964, because of material changes since made to valves.

To achieve correct valve timing, place a dial test indicator (DTI) on number one piston by mounting it on the head and inserting an extension through the number one plug hole. Rotate the engine anti-clockwise a little, then clockwise, until the dial pointer reaches a maximum. Note the reading—this denotes the

The inlet valve has hit the top of the piston (note the shiny mark in the cut-out), due to incorrect valve timing

true top-dead-centre position. Attach the timing disc to the crankshaft and set a pointer on the front cover; zero the timing to this pointer. Place the DTI on number four exhaust tappet, and measure the maximum opening point (MOP) of the camshaft. The exhaust should always be measured first because of the fixed length of chain between the crankshaft and exhaust sprockets. Turn the engine in the normal direction of rotation until the pointer on the DTI reaches a maximum. Note the reading in degrees on the timing disc. Continue turning until the pointer moves again, and note this reading.

To calculate the true MOP of any camshaft (if unknown), use the following formula:

Example 1—standard B-type camshaft

Inlet valve

Opens	22 degrees BTDC (before top dead centre)
Closes	62 degrees ABDC (after bottom dead centre)

Exhaust valve

Opens	62 degrees BBDC (before bottom dead centre)
Closes	22 degrees ATDC (after top dead centre)

For the inlet camshaft with 22/62 settings:

add 22 + 62 = 84
add 180 = 264
divide by 2 = 132
subtract 22 = 110 (MOP)

Inlet will be fully open at 110 degrees ATDC.

For exhaust camshaft with 62/22 settings:

add 62 + 22 = 84
add 180 = 264
divide by 2 = 132
subtract 22 = 110 (MOP)

Exhaust will be fully open at 110 degrees BTDC.

Example 2—S/E and Sprint C- and D-type camshaft

Inlet valve

Opens	26 degrees BTDC
Closes	66 degrees ABDC

Exhaust valve

Opens	66 degrees BBDC
Closes	26 degrees ATDC

For the inlet camshaft with 26/66 settings:
add 26 + 66 = 92
add 180 = 272
divide by 2 = 136
subtract 26 = 110 (MOP)
Inlet will be fully open 110 degrees ATDC.

For the exhaust camshaft with 66/26 settings:
add 66 + 26· = 92
add 180 = 272
divide by 2 = 136
subtract 26 = 110 (MOP)
Exhaust will be fully open 110 degrees BTDC.

Example 3—L2 camshaft (138–140 bhp)
Inlet valve
Opens 46 degrees BTDC
Closes 70 degrees ABDC
Exhaust valve
Opens 70 degrees BBDC
Closes 46 degrees ATDC

For the inlet with 46/70 settings:
add 46 + 70 = 116
add 180 = 296
divide by 2 = 148
subtract 46 = 102 (MOP)
Inlet will be fully open at 102 degrees ATDC.

For the exhaust with 70/46 settings:
add 70 + 46 = 116
add 180 = 296
divide by 2 = 148
subtract 46 = 102 (MOP)
Exhaust will be fully open at 102 degrees BTDC.

The valve clearance on the L2 camshaft is set at 0.010 in. inlet, 0.010 in. exhaust. Any camshaft MOP can be worked out using this formula, but the valve angles must always be known.

Taking the Sprint (D-type) camshaft as the working example, the true MOP, as calculated, is 110 degrees (for both camshafts, since they are identical). From the DTI, the readings on the timing disc gave 107.5 degrees and 112.5 degrees—a difference of 5 degrees. Divide this by

Establishing true top dead centre (TDC) before fitting the head (see text). If the head has already been installed, fit an extension on the DTI, and gain access to the top of the piston through number one spark plug hole. Note the pointer bolted to the front cover, by the dipstick tube. The disc must be zeroed to this

2, adding the result (2.5 degrees) to the minimum reading, and subtracting it from the maximum reading, to achieve the actual MOP:
107.5 + 2.5 = 110 degrees
112.5 − 2.5 = 110 degrees
Therefore, the true MOP is equal to the actual MOP and, consequently, is correct, so the original sprocket dowel is retained.

Still using the Sprint camshaft as an example, assume readings of 104.5 and 111.5 degrees were obtained—a difference of 7 degrees.
7 ÷ 2 = 3.5 degrees
104.5 + 3.5 = 108 degrees
111.5 − 3.5 = 108 degrees
Therefore, the true MOP does not equal the actual MOP, so it is incorrect by 2 degrees.

Applying the same figures to the L2 camshaft will give a true MOP of 102 degrees compared with an actual MOP of 108 degrees.

In both cases, the use of offset dowels is necessary to achieve the correct timing.

With the D-type cam, there is a 2-degree error at the crankshaft. This is divided by two to give the error at the camshaft, i.e. 1 degree. The offset required is 1 degree multiplied by a constant (0.012). Therefore, the offset dowel size is 0.012. In the L2-camshaft example, there is a 6-degree error at the crankshaft, giving a 3-degree error at the camshaft. The degree of offset equals 3 degrees multiplied by 0.012 to give 0.036.

Remove the standard dowel in the camshaft and insert the offset dowel, making sure that it is located correctly—it will only fit in two positions, 180 degrees apart. It must lie on the pitch-circle diameter, otherwise the sprocket will not fit over the camshaft. Replace the sprocket and the timing chain (to the correct tension) and check the MOP again. The true figure should now equal the actual figure.

Having established the correct timing for the exhaust camshaft, repeat the operation exactly for the inlet camshaft, turning the crankshaft to TDC and placing the DTI on number four inlet lobe to find the actual MOP.

As an example, with the Sprint camshaft, assume timing-disc readings of 106.5 and 111.5 degrees—a difference of 5 degrees.
5 ÷ 2 = 2.5 degrees
106.5 + 2.5 = 109 degrees
111.5 − 2.5 = 109 degrees
Therefore, the actual MOP is 109 degrees and there is a 1-degree error at the crankshaft, or 0.5 degree at the camshaft. The degree of offset

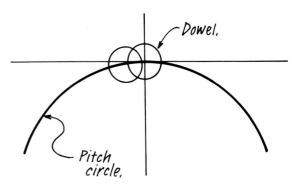

Above
When fitting an offset dowel, it must lie on the pitch-circle diameter

Left
The DTI on number four cam follower to establish the maximum lift, and hence the true MOP

required is 0.5 multiplied by 0.012, which comes to 0.006. Fit an offset dowel, as before, reassemble and check. Both inlet and exhaust timing should now be spot on.

NOTE For a road engine, a 2-degree error at the crankshaft (i.e. a 1-degree error at the camshaft) is acceptable—in fact, the engine probably will not notice!

The 0.012 constant used in the calculations is derived mathematically: K (the constant) equals the radius between the dowel centre and camshaft centre divided by 57.3. K is measured in inches/crankshaft degree. The offset dowels are graded in thousandths of an inch and correspond to the following crankshaft errors:

Degrees at crankshaft	Offset dowel
1	0.006
2	0.012
3	0.018
4	0.024
5	0.030
6	0.036
7	0.042
8	0.048
9	0.054
10	0.060

No offset is greater than 0.060 in. because the sprocket can be turned by one tooth if necessary, to give 10 degrees at the crankshaft. Since there are 34 teeth on the sprocket, each tooth represents 10.588 degrees. Therefore, to correct a 10-degree error at the crankshaft, i.e. 5 degrees at the camshaft, the sprocket is moved by one tooth and a smaller offset dowel, say 0.006, may be used if needed.

Many firms make offset dowels—those made by Cosworth are quality assured. Some firms offer vernier wheels which replace the standard camshaft sprockets and provide adjustment by means of the pitch difference between the holes in the cam wheel and the holes in the front cam-sprocket washer. It is essential to know the amount of offset that each hole represents. The vernier wheels obviously cost considerably more than offset dowels, and some of those presently on offer in the UK are badly machined, so choose carefully if you decide to take this route.

Having completed the valve timing, apply new timing marks to the sprockets with a fine brush or etching pen, resting it on a thin plate laid on the head and butted up to the sprockets. Then proceed with the rest of the rebuild as normal.

6 Carburettors

There are three requirements for an engine to perform properly—compression, fuel and ignition—so it becomes irrelevant that the engine has been rebuilt to the highest standard imaginable if the carburettor and/or distributor are worn out. An engine can only be as good as the distribution of fuel and sparks. Accordingly, before the engine is run, make sure these two items are in perfect order.

Weber and Dellorto carburettors give little trouble but, due to their age, Webers (some over 20 years old) may have corroded internal drillings caused by water in the fuel, or may be silted up with lead. If this is the case, the bodies must be scrapped. Jet bleed is common with age, too. It occurs when the jet has been consistently overtightened into the body, causing distortion and hence fuel leakage—again the bodies must be scrapped. Gaskets and O-rings may have perished, which allows fuel and air leakage. If in any doubt, renew the carburettor completely, otherwise make sure that the chokes and jets match the specification tables given in this book; fit new gaskets and reset the float level correctly. Do not fit Type 18 and Type 31 Webers to the same engine, as the internal drillings are different.

Dellortos can be approached in the same way as Webers, but special attention must be paid to the accelerator-pump mechanism and the diaphragm. New Dellortos are cheaper than new Webers, and many Big Valve engines have benefited from being fitted with new Dellortos; fuel consumption decreases dramatically.

Strombergs require more attention, since there is a fine difference between correct and diabolical performance. As already outlined, with the S/E engines, the high-compression head causes problems—now—with pinking being more likely due to the leaner running of the carburettor. The Strombergs should have their diaphragms changed every year (originally, this was specified for every 12,000-mile service), since fuel and oil can perish or distort them. No air leakage must occur, either through the adaptor-block O-ring or, more commonly now (due to age), through the throttle spindles and seals. Any air leakage will cause an even leaner mixture, to the detriment of smooth running. Like Webers and Dellortos, if there is any serious internal corrosion, the bodies must be renewed, and this also applies to distorted spindle locations. If in any doubt, the Strombergs must be rebuilt completely, using new gaskets, needles, O-rings and spindles (the last may require sleeving of the bodies).

The O-ring at the base of the air valve/needle may allow the damper oil to drain away quickly, which gives rise to flat spots and hesitation. It must be in perfect order, as must the O-ring at the base of the float chamber to prevent fuel leakage. Do not fiddle with temperature compensators—if in any doubt as to their function, replace them.

On the domestic market, much controversy surrounded the function of the high-level balance pipe. It was said to improve the idle characteristics and help prevent the icing problem. This was total rubbish, since the idle characteristics were caused by the layout of the head and the camshaft design, while icing was due to the air speed increasing as it passed the needle. The real reason for the change was that neat fuel was found to be settling in the low-level pipe which, as Graham Atkin pointed out, 'was not a very satisfactory state of affairs', hence the use of a high-level pipe. Perhaps Lotus tried to sell the high-level pipe through dealers as a 'gain', rather than admit to a potential fire hazard. Many Strombergs still have

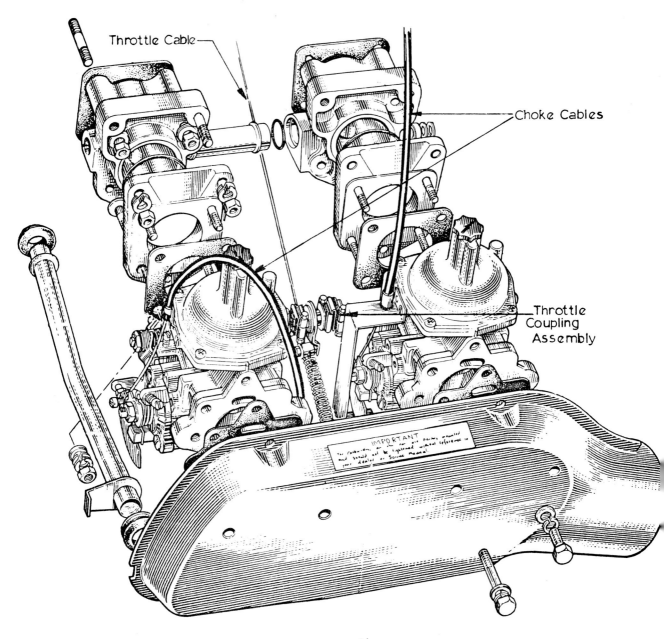

Throttle Cable

Choke Cables

Throttle
Coupling
Assembly

IMPORTANT

Above
Here is the arrangement of Zenith-Stromberg carburettors as used on domestic-market twin-cams. This particular installation has the low-level balance pipe

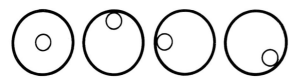

Fixed needles should be constantly in the centre of the jet (far left), but in reality they could be in any position, as shown in the remaining three examples, leading to erratic fuel metering

Right
This 'exploded' drawing from the Lotus manual shows every detail of the Zenith-Stromberg carburettors used on exhaust-emission Lotus twin-cams

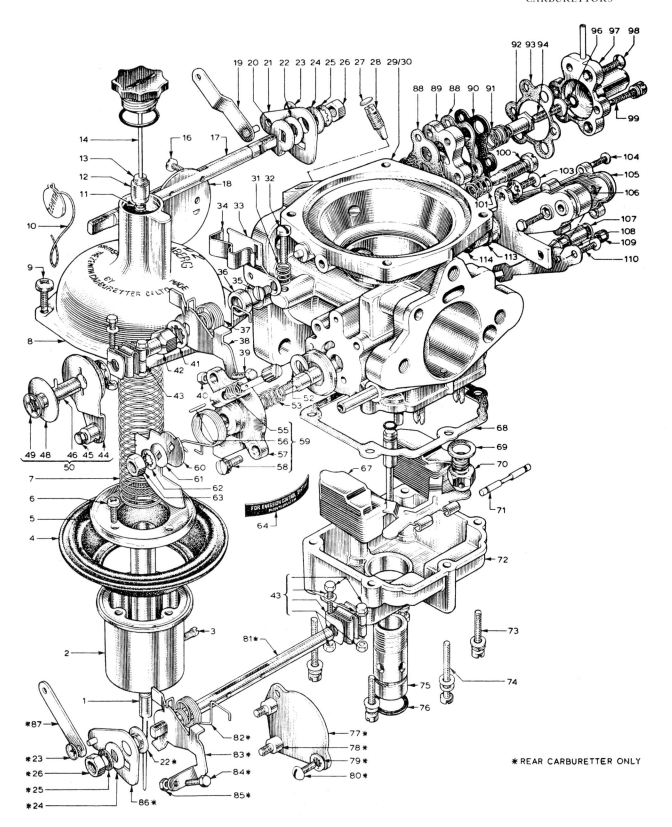

* REAR CARBURETTER ONLY

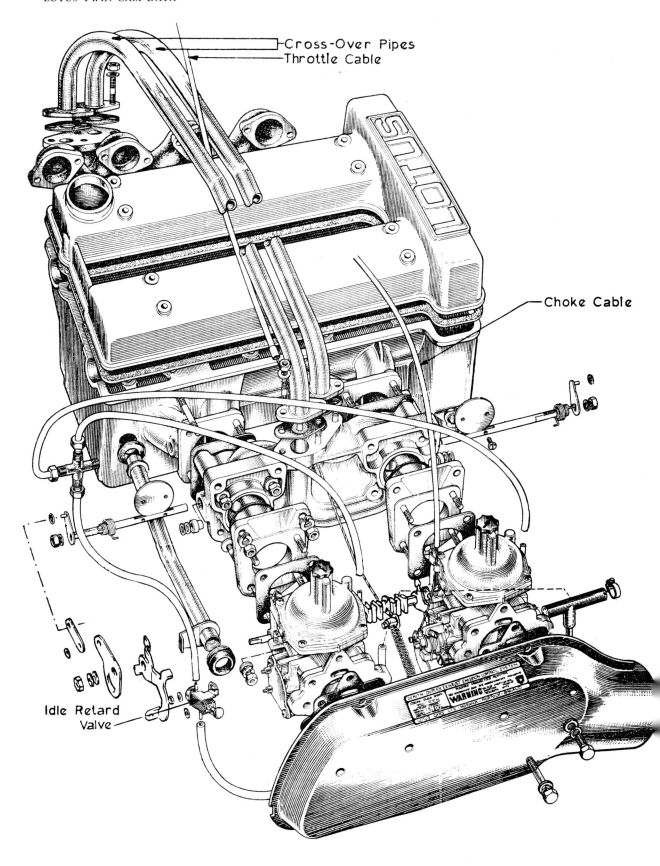

Cross-Over Pipes
Throttle Cable

Choke Cable

Idle Retard
Valve

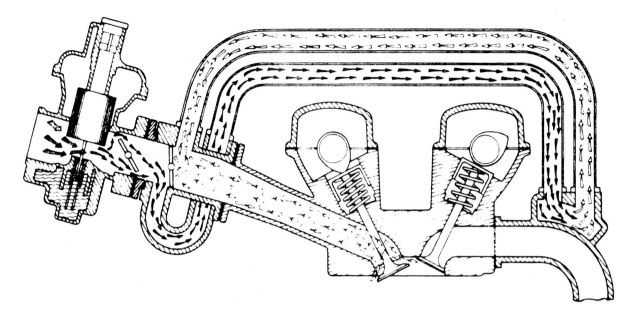

their low-level pipes and have suffered no ill effects at all.

The original fixed BIY needle did not work well, since it could, and did, lie in any place, giving rise to inconsistent fuel metering. The move to the floating needle, which was biased in one position to give a consistent condition, was to overcome this irregular metering. In the latest reprinted workshop manuals, Lotus state that a BIY floating needle was used with a low-level pipe, and a 2 BAR floating needle with a high-level pipe. Once again, this is misleading, since the 2 BAR was fitted to carburettors with low-level pipes (my own Elan, in March 1970, had this arrangement). No one can recall seeing a BIY floating needle at the factory—the change was from BIY fixed to 2 BAR floating, irrespective of balance pipes.

The emission engines require even more stringent care of their Strombergs, not only to ensure that no air or fuel leakage takes place, but also that the cross-over pipes are bolted down completely true. The Lotus workshop manual explains the theoretical workings of these carburettors, and the system of emission control in general, but it does not explain the practical application, allied to poor performance. The idea

When Zenith-Stromberg carburettors were used for exhaust-emission twin-cams, the installation looked like this

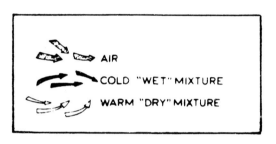

Cross-over pipes were used to give a degree of preheat to the air/fuel mixture on exhaust-emission cars

of preheating the fuel mixture is to reduce hydrocarbon levels. However, there were two reasons for poor performance. Firstly, the ignition timing was responsible for the low- and high-speed problems (a different distributor was fitted to US-specification cars); secondly, the transition phase between primary and secondary throttles at 40 degrees gave monumental flat-spot characteristics.

In theory, the performance of an emission engine at full throttle opening should revert to that of a normal domestic engine, but in reality, once the low-speed problems (up to 60 mph) had been overcome, the delay was so long that most people forgot that there was any top-end performance! The Stromberg emission engines are not looked upon with great fondness but, as usual with Lotus, if the time and finance had been available, these problems would have been overcome. The only 'cure' for these engines is a return to standard UK specification, i.e. to fit adaptor blocks, balance pipe, 175 CDS Strombergs, four-branch manifold and a distributor, all of which is illegal in the USA.

With all carburettor installations, make sure that there are no air or vacuum leaks through distorted O-rings, vacuum take-offs for brake servos, headlamps, and distributor (rear emission Stromberg only). Also, on emission Strombergs and ECE 15-specification Dellortos, make sure there are no air leaks on the ignition-retard capsule pipes.

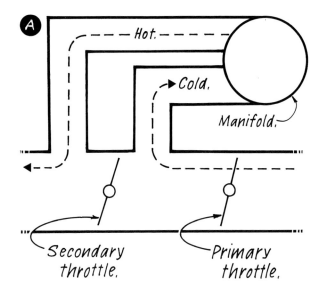

Operation of primary and secondary throttles in Stromberg emission carburettors:
A   At up to 30 degrees throttle openingl the system functions correctly and all cold mixture is heated
B   At 40 degrees throttle opening, cold mixture is still preheated, but some manages to pass the secondary throttle, giving rise to poor distribution and running
C   At 82 degrees throttle opening, the arrangement reverts to the normal UK specification, with no mixture being preheated

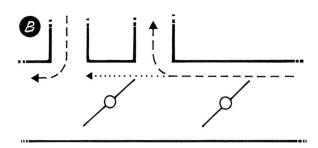

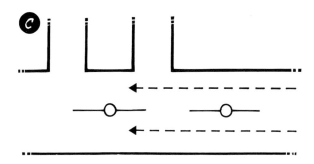

7 Ignition

Distributors

No fewer than five different distributors were used on the twin-cam, all with varying degrees of advance. Since they all appeared to function on the same basic engine, how could they work correctly with as much as 12 degrees difference in advance between them? Unfortunately, once again, the various workshop manuals are misleading, and the earlier manuals are wrong.

Before unravelling the complexities, and explaining why different distributors were used, one particular aspect must be cleared up, namely that Lucas distributors 23D4 and 25D4 were current at the same time. The 25D4 had a vacuum retard mechanism, while the 23D4 did not. The early 25D4 (as stated in the workshop manuals) is not the same as the late emission/European 25D4. Distributors used by Lotus on the twin-cam engine are shown in the table below.

Model	Number	Introduced	Ignition advance (distributor degrees)	Engine use
23D4	40953	18 September 1963	11–13	Standard Weber, Elan, L/Cortina. All domestic Strombergs on Elan, +2, Europa
23D4	41189A	6 March 1967	6–8	All S/E engines on Elan, +2, Europa, L/Cortina S/E, Escort T/Cam, all domestic Big Valve engines
25D4	40930	early 1962–63 (ceased early 1964)	12–13	1498 cc T/Cam, early 1558 cc T/Cam on Elan, L/Cortina
25D4	41225A	3 January 1968	6–8	Federal exhaust-emission Strombergs only—all types, Big Valve Dellorto, domestic and European, ECE 15 regulations
25D4	41225 (vacuum retard removed)		6–8	European, late-model domestic Big Valve engines, pre ECE 15 regulations

The current production Lotus/Lucas distributor model is 43D4, which is a direct replacement for 41189 and 41225 only.

The static ignition-timing settings listed in the different manuals vary, but the true static settings are as follows:

Engine use	Distributor	Static setting (degrees BTDC)
1498 cc, early 1558 cc Weber (B-type cam)	40930	7
All Weber standard (B-type cam)	40953	12
All Stromberg domestic (C/D-type cam)	40953	9
All S/E Weber (C-type cam)	41189A	10
All Big Valve Weber/Dellorto domestic (D-type cam)	41189A	12
All Stromberg Federal emission (C/D/E-type cam)	41225A	5
All European-specification Dellorto (ECE 15 regulations) (C/D-type cam)	41225A	5
All Big Valve Dellorto, domestic and European, pre ECE 15 regs	41225	10

Now to detail: the advance curves for all types. Please note that in the manuals, Lotus get confused between crankshaft rpm and distributor rpm. Distributor rpm is half crankshaft rpm; in some cases, static settings have been added, in others they have not! The following tables are the final settings, i.e. static settings have been added, so maximum advance is exactly what it says.

40953 distributor rpm	Standard Weber (B-type cam)	All Stromberg Domestic (C/D-type cam)
Below 500	12.0	9.0
Below 1000	static, no advance	static, no advance
1000	17.6	14.6
1500	22.5	19.5
2000	28.0	25.0
2500	28.8	25.8
3000	29.8	26.8
3500	30.6	27.6
4000	31.5	28.5
4500	32.5	29.5
5000	33.5	30.5
5500	34.5	31.5
6000	35.5	32.5
6500	36.0	33.0
	maximum advance	

41189A distributor rpm	All S/E Weber (C-type cam)	All Big Valve Weber/Dellorto Domestic (D-type cam)
Below 2000	10.0 static, no advance	12.0 static, no advance
2500	12.5	14.5
3000	14.5	16.5
3500	17.0	19.0
4000	19.3	21.3
4500	21.5	23.5
5000–6500	24.0	26.0
		maximum advance

41225 distributor rpm	European Dellorto only* (C/D-type cam)
Below 1000	10.0 static, no advance
2000	15.0
2500	17.4
3000	19.6
3500	21.8
4000	24.2
4500	26.6
5000–6500	29.0
	maximum advance

*Also some very late domestic—replacement for 41189.

168

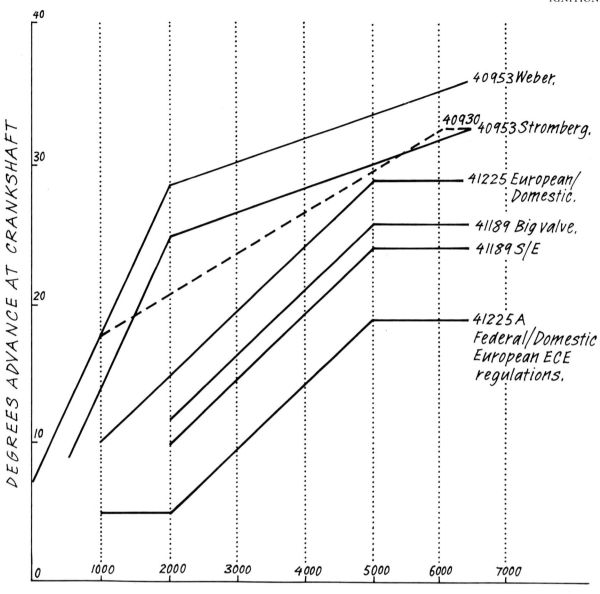

Distributor advance characteristics

41225A distributor rpm	All Federal Stromberg Domestic/ European ECE 15 spec. (C/D/E-type cam) Vacuum retard capsule fitted
Below 2000	5.0 static, no advance
2500	7.5
3000	9.5
3500	12.0
4000	14.3
4500	16.5
5000–6500	19.0 maximum advance

LOTUS SERVICE BULLETIN

LOTUS CARS Ltd NORWICH NORFOLK NOR92W   Tel: WYMONDHAM 3411   CABLES LOTUS NORWICH   TELEX 97401

Class	111
Number	1973/33
Type	+2'S130'&Europa
Date	02.11.73

Circulation List	Service Manager		Foreman				

Title: European Exhaust Emission.

Reason: To advise Dealer personnel of parts involved when above Specification (E.C.E.15) is fitted.

Parts Required:

R026 S 0710W	Carburetter (DHLA 4OE)	1 off
G026 M 0009W	Distributor	1 off
A036 E 0837W	Vacuum pipe	1 off

Action:

1. Commencing at the following Chassis Numbers, all cars manufactured and intended for use on, or after 10th. November 1973, are required by Law to conform to this Specification:

Elan +2 'S130'

73101689L	)	
73101696L	)	
73101700L	)	
73101703L	)	Gt. Britain & N. Ireland
73101706L	)	
73101711L onwards	)	
73100335M	)	Export

Europa 'Special'

| 73112229P |) | Gt. Britain & N. Ireland |
| 73111304Q |) | Export |

2. With the above Specification, ignition timing and slow running speeds are altered to:

Ignition timing (static)	10° B.T.D.C.
Ignition timing (at idle)	5° B.T.D.C.
Slow running speed (idle)	900/1,000 r.p.m.

Distributor Centrifugal Advance

Below 1,000	)	5.0	)	
1,250	)	7.4	)	
1,500	) Crankshaft	9.6	)	Crankshaft
1,750	) r.p.m.	11.8	)	degrees
2,000	)	14.2	)	B.T.D.C.
2,250	)	16.6	)	
2,500	)	19.0	)	– MAXIMUM advance

Above
The Lotus/Lucas 43D4 replacement distributor for the 41189 and 41225 types. The cap is screwed on. The 'L' stands for Lotus, and was incorporated into the casting, together with other changes, in 1967

Left
ECE 15 ignition-timing and advance specifications

All the settings given may need slight adjustment to meet local fuel requirements and, because of the demise of 101 RM octane fuel, the domestic Big Valve settings should be decreased by 2 degrees, i.e. the static set at 10 degrees and maximum advance at 24 degrees. Use the S/E figures for the 41189A. European and domestic 41225 may also require dropping back to 8 degrees static, 27 degrees maximum. Do not reduce the static setting by more than 2 degrees on any distributor.

It is strange that the Weber standard and S/E versions differ by 12 degrees maximum advance and, as Graham Atkin and John Bloomfield pointed out, 'No Weber twin-cam engine specification needs more than 24–25 degrees of advance, whereas the Stromberg does.' As to the reason, it can only be surmised that the 41189 was not available (service introduced on 6 March 1967, but original equipment from Lucas would be supplied a few months before this), and the early 40930 and 40953 (18 September 1963) were. Possibly because of the function of the standard cam profiles, the twin-cam performed correctly, but with the introduction of the S/E (C-type cam) did not require so much advance. Presumably, it ran well enough until the 41189 was introduced to restore the balance. One thing is quite certain, the Big Valve must **not** have the 40953 distributor fitted, otherwise severe pinking will occur due to the engine being so over-advanced. All S/E engines should be fitted with the 41189, but up to 1967 the 40953 was fitted. This should now be changed for the current 43D4 model to improve the general running of these engines. This would apply only to S/E engines, i.e. any Elan or Lotus-Cortina built before 1967. After that date, all S/E engines had the 41189—only those +2s and Europas with Stromberg carburettors had the 40953 distributor.

The Stromberg engines required more advance, hence a 33-degree maximum (domestic), to overcome the deficiencies of the carburettor. However, on the domestic S/E engines, as has been pointed out, with the increased compression, the high maximum advance does not help an engine trying to cope with 99-octane fuel, leaner and hotter running, and a cylinder head which has been skimmed. This engine now tends to give the same characteristics as a Big Valve with a 40953 distributor. Retarding the ignition drastically—to restrict maximum advance—is not the answer, and fitting a 41189 distributor is an even worse solution, since it does not give enough maximum advance. As there is no replacement available for the 40953 (after all, the other engines can all run on 41189 or 41225), the only way out is to set the static to 7 degrees BTDC, giving 31 degrees maximum. Although the 41225 in European guise gives 29 degrees maximum advance, the advance curve is completely different (see graph) from that of the 40953, and the Stromberg requires advance from 5000 rpm onwards. Without doubt, the Stromberg engine is the odd one out as regards distributors.

The Federal Stromberg engine is difficult to satisfy, since its 5-degree static setting was found to be the best for an early warm-up (and a quicker reduction in HC levels), and the initial advance curve was ideal for the emission laws. However, with a listed maximum of 19 degrees, the engine could not possibly run properly. After all, the domestic engine must have its 33-degree maximum, which is a far cry from 19 degrees. The explanation is that to overcome the restrictions placed upon the engine by the emission controls, the distributor curve was set to give the optimum performance in the low rpm range where, of course, the control was placed, because the Strombergs reverted to the domestic arrangement after 3000–3500 rpm. That is not to say that, 'in the field', the static setting was increased somewhat to supplement the poor performance.

A figure given in earlier manuals (albeit against the wrong distributor!) was 12 degrees BTDC—in fact, the static could be raised as high as 14–15 degrees to give a maximum advance of 28–29 degrees on the 41225A. This helps, of course, but the maximum advance then stops at 5000 rpm, not at the 6500 rpm of the 40953 on the domestic engines. As I have stated, time and again, with extra finance and time Lotus would have overcome this, but they had to do their best with the limited resources and parts available. Regretably, Federal engines accounted for only a

small percentage of the total number produced and, at the time, to put these right may have appeared to be wasted expense, particularly as sales were declining (into 1971) in the USA and more important projects (like the new 907 engines) were under way.

The 41225, for pre ECE 15 European-specification engines with Dellortos, required the slightly higher maximum advance to overcome the restrictions placed on the carburettors by their smaller chokes (see carburettor table). These engines leant towards the domestic Stromberg with the volumetric restrictions, as opposed to the normal Weber and Dellorto engines.

With all types of distributor, it is essential that they are in perfect working order. Due to age, most are now very worn, giving totally unrepresentative advance curves and destroying the engine's capabilities—with low- and high-speed pinking, piston damage and head damage (pock marking) all resulting. The easy check is with the timing light, making sure that the advance curve follows the tables given to a tolerance of ± 2 degrees. A full advance reading at 1500 rpm means the distributor is worn out and must be rebuilt (difficult, since there are no parts), or replaced by the 43D4 model for the 41189/41225. Do not continue to use a worn out distributor, for a new one restores the engine to its former glory, giving instant response. At present, the 40953 type can only be salvaged by building a 'new' one from several old ones. Perhaps if there is sufficient demand, Lucas/Lotus may produce a distributor with the same characteristics.

Electronic ignition was never fitted as a factory option by Lotus—no twin-cam engined car ever left Hethel with transistorized ignition. However, many owners fitted this after delivery and, apart from the usual benefits on the twin-cam, it also reduces distributor wear and avoids the need to remove the distributor when changing the contact points. Make sure any electronic system (whether fitted or about to be fitted) is compatible with the engine and electrical polarity of the car, and that it is also compatible with the rev counter. One of the best types, which does not disturb the rev counter, is the Lucas electronic unit (introduced in 1985). With electronic ignition fitted, a common mistake is to neglect to lubricate the bobbin-weight spindles, thus causing the advance mechanism to stick and give an incorrect advance curve. Another benefit of electronic ignition is that the ignition timing will not alter as it does with

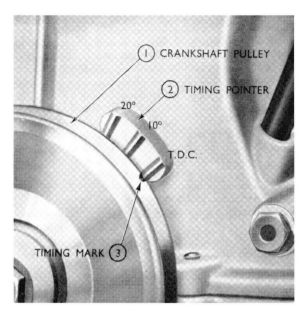

An early type of engine front cover, showing TDC, 10-degree and 20-degree marks only; the 30-degree mark was added for later engines

conventional ignition due to increased heel wear on the contact breaker.

Distributor data: all models

Firing order	1-3-4-2
Firing angles (degrees)	0-90-180-270 ($\pm$ 1)
Contact-points gap	0.014–0.016 in.
	(0.35–0.40 mm)
Contact-lever spring tension	18–24 oz
	(0.51–0.68 kg)
Dwell angle (degrees)	60 ($\pm$ 3)
Rotor-arm cut-out	
Big Valve	6750 rpm
all others	6500 rpm
Direction of rotation	Anti-clockwise
Contact-gap check	Every 3000 miles
Contact-points change	Every 6000 miles

Sparking plugs

Originally, Autolite plugs were used because of the contract with Ford, and because Ford owned that company. Autolite became Autocraft, and is now Motorcraft. However, Champion plugs are universally known, and are listed below. Bosch, NGK and Motorcraft equivalents can be cross-referred if required.

Application	Champion plug	Gap
Federal	N9Y* (N9Yc)	0.025 in.
Stromberg		(0.6 mm)
All others	N7Y (N7Yc)	0.020–0.023 in.
		(0.55 mm)

*For sustained high speed revert to N7Y.

With electronic ignition:		
All types	N7Y (N7Yc)	0.030–0.035 in.
	or	(0.8 mm)
	N6Y (N6Yc)	

If resistive leads are fitted (as on the 2 litre or 2.2 litre series), use RN7Y or RN6Y plugs with electronic ignition. Electronic ignition provides a high voltage and a hotter, fatter spark, hence the need for a wider gap and 'colder' plug.

For normal driving, Federal Stromberg engines require a 'hotter' plug to ensure a complete burn of fuel, as a 'cold' plug may leave traces of unburnt fuel, thus increasing the hydro-carbon levels. However, for sustained high-speed running the 'hotter' plug electrode will be damaged by the heat and a 'colder' plug must be used.

Never deviate from this list of plugs (for instance, permanently oiled-up plugs will not benefit from a change of grade—always rectify the cause first). The plug listed will always be correct.

One last point on ignition: on early front covers there is no 30-degree mark, but only TDC, 10 degrees and 20 degrees. For advance-curve purposes, therefore, paint on the 30-degree mark with the aid of a protractor aligned on the TDC, 10-degree and 20-degree marks. It is strange that, with the high initial advance of the 40953 distributor, this was never done in the first place.

8 Air filtration and silencing

The wrong type of air filtration or exhaust silencing can severely restrict the power output and general running of the twin-cam engine. Many specialists have recommended their own 'correct' air-filtration systems, but however hard one might try to justify these systems compared with the correct Lotus version, there really seems to be no improvement. The Lotus system was evolved to give a good cold air flow within the practical limits of design and space available for the necessary canisters and trunking. By making use of the backplate, the throttle linkage makes a very neat installation.

The original brochures of the Elan 1500 and 1600 showed a bolt-on air filter across the trumpets, but with no throttle installation! It is essential that the trumpets are always covered because of the fire risk due to backfires and the volume of dust and grit that will otherwise be sucked into the engine. Without an air box, fuel will persistently spit back, soak into the inner wings and could eventually ignite—the paint burns first, followed by the GRP. An air box, although made of GRP, will prevent a fire occurring because of its enclosed space. With 'pancake' filters fitted, there is no power loss, but these are sucking in hot air; on Lotus models all the engine-bay air is ducted through the radiators—Europas have a higher ambient temperature in the engine bay anyway. The Cortina/Escort models have 'proper' radiators and greatly-enlarged air space around the engines.

With the correct system in use, the trunking must not be split, otherwise it loses its effectiveness. The air filter must be clean (change it every 12,000 miles/20,000 km). The engine will run best on cold, clean air, which is slightly moist. The air box must also be sealed, and not split or broken. If this happens, renew both the metal backplate and the air box with its seal. Petrol can drip over the starter motor and be a potential fire hazard.

Race engines work to different standards, as will be apparent throughout this book, in that they are stripped and rebuilt every year, or perhaps more frequently.

A correct exhaust system is also very important—the wrong diameter pipes and silencers will impair performance, while incorrect silencer baffling will cause back pressure which, in turn, will cause an engine to almost stop. Lotus went to great lengths to get the pipe diameters and baffling correct. Do not alter the systems. The changes made during the engine's (car's) life were made because of increased knowledge and efficiency, which means that all early Elans and +2s will benefit from the use of the later fabricated, four-branch manifold, instead of the original cast-iron version (which is now obsolete). The transverse silencers were necessary to fit below existing body moulds, and the later straight-through types were very efficient, the S4 twin-box system being the most efficient of all. The change to the Sprint type was made for two reasons—one was because it helped the styling; the other was because the twin-box system tended to blow out its baffles very quickly.

The advent of 'after-market' stainless-steel systems has caused many problems—most of those on offer for the Lotus twin-cam range are pure rubbish with wrong diameters and incorrect construction, which gives rise to back pressure and noise. Worst of all, these systems do not last long, because of the thin gauge of stainless steel used—they actually craze and break up due to internal corrosion. A proper system made from the correct grade of stainless steel will last for ever, and be of great benefit, provided it is done to the original Lotus drawings. However, as with the water-pump conundrum, more and more owners are reverting to the original mild-steel Lotus systems for peace of mind. A point worth remembering is that all Lotus exhaust systems (both twin-cam and modern) are made under licence to original drawings; they cannot be bought anywhere in the world, except from Lotus dealers. Any other exhaust system which you find on offer is not genuine, even though it may be advertised as such. The wrong system can rob the engine of anything up to 15 bhp—this has been proved by dynamometer power tests. The latest (1987) Esprit S/E drops 8 bhp compared with the Excel S/E, purely because of its different exhaust system, although the engine is otherwise identical.

This extract from an Elan 1500 brochure shows the bolt-on air filter

Fantastic acceleration combining with amazing docility

The engine of the Lotus Elan is a completely new design, yet it has combined traditional Ford reliability and low running costs with the brilliant and exclusive Lotus twin overhead camshaft light alloy cylinder head already proven in international motor competition. The Lotus Elan has a short stroke engine, with five crankshaft main bearings, yielding high torque and power at low piston speeds. This results in long life and remarkable smoothness of operation throughout the engine's entire rev. range. Specifically designed and developed to provide really sparkling performance with quiet trouble free operation, Lotus and Ford are combined in the production of the most advanced and successful light sports car engine in the world.

9 Running-in

Finally, some advice on running-in procedures. Fill the engine with oil—use a good-quality 15W–50 or 20W–50 product from a well-known manufacturer, such as Duckhams, Castrol, Shell, Esso or BP—but **never** use cheap oil; it is cheap because it contains fewer, if any, beneficial additives.

The alternative is to use a synthetic oil, such as that made by Mobil. Do not mix the two types. If using a synthetic oil, always stay faithful to it—the benefits are that the engine stays cleaner, and that the oil lasts longer. However, synthetic oils are far more expensive than conventional mineral oils. Do not use any additives, for the Graphogen used on assembly will protect the engine on initial start-up and running. The use of proprietary additives will hinder the bedding-in process because of their 'super slide' properties. Fill the sump to above the dipstick maximum to allow for the capacity of the filter.

Next, pour in warm water and antifreeze mixture to a 20–25 per cent strength, which is ample for normal, year round operation above freezing point; for UK winter conditions increase the strength to 30 per cent. For the USA and Canada increase the winter strength to 50–60 per cent and use a thinner oil, say 10W-40.

NOTE The twin-cam engine will not run properly on lead-free petrol, and great harm will be done if you attempt to run the car on this type of fuel. Because the valve seats are cast-iron (unlike the 2/2.2 litre series, which are of sintered material), they will be progressively eroded; damage will also be caused to the valves and to the piston crowns.

If, in the future, lead-free fuel becomes standard (which must surely never happen, otherwise all classic cars are in danger of being forced off the road), then the twin-cam owner will have to use additives, which are already available. These serve to raise the octane level to the present ratings of fuel which contains lead additives.

Remove the spark plugs and crank the engine on the starter until the fuel rises in the mechanical fuel-pump bowl. Prime the carburettors (if an electric pump is fitted, the carburettors will be primed automatically) and check for any fuel leaks. If there are no leaks, continue cranking for a few seconds. Replace the plugs and HT leads. With Webers, pump the throttle three or four times, but with Dellortos and Strombergs, use full choke; operate the starter. The engine should fire immediately. If not, pump again (Webers) and try once more. Immediately the engine fires, check for oil pressure and that there are no leaks. Check the ignition timing immediately, with a strobe timing light, and reset it to the correct figure if necessary. Now run the engine at a fast idle (1500–1800 rpm) for five to ten minutes, checking the mixtures and the carburettor balance. Switch off and let everything settle, then check the oil and water levels. There is **no need** to re-torque the head when it is cold—this is never necessary.

When all the engine settings are correct, the start-up procedures are as follows:

Cold engine

Webers—three or four pumps and no choke. On very cold days (at −5 degrees Celsius and below), use the choke.

Dellortos—use full choke. Do not pump the throttle, for these carburettors do not operate in the same way as the Webers. (Unfortunately, some modern twin-cams have been blown up because their owners kept pumping away, thinking that their Dellortos looked the same as

Webers—this fills the air box with neat fuel, and if a flash-back occurs there will be an explosion). As soon as the engine starts, progressively push in the choke and begin to use the throttle.

Strombergs—use full choke. Do not pump the throttle, as this serves no purpose whatsoever. On very cold days, choke may be required for two or three miles before the engine begins to warm up.

Warm engine

All carburettors—simply turn the key and the engine will start immediately. Do not pump the throttle, otherwise flooding will occur.

When hot

All carburettors—depress the throttle pedal to its limit and hold it there. Crank the engine (up to eight, or even ten times) until it fires, then release the pedal immediately. Do not pump the throttle under any circumstances, otherwise the engine will never start and a lengthy wait will be needed until it cools off.

On the road, do not exceed 3000 rpm in any gear for the first 1000 miles (1600 km). Do not use full throttle and do not let the engine 'labour' in any gear. After 1000 miles, increase the speed by 500 rpm for every extra 500 miles (800 km), with short bursts of wider throttle openings. The twin-cam will not be fully run-in until at least 3000 miles (4800 km) have been completed. Running-in is very important to ensure that everything beds in correctly—look after the engine and the performance will be maintained for at least 60,000 miles (96,000 km). The engine life is good for 80–90,000 miles (128–144,000 km) before bearings have to be replaced.

After the first 500 miles, change the oil and the filter; after 1000 miles, check the valve clearances and timing-chain tension. Re-torque the head/front-cover bolts as the cork gasket compresses. Change the oil and the filter every 3000 miles. If the annual mileage covered is very small, change the oil at least twice a year, irrespective of miles covered. Running the engine only occasionally will still cause the acids in the oil to attack the bearings etc. Starting the engine in the garage during winter and running it for a few minutes does more harm than good—do not do it. Either leave it alone, or run it up to normal operating temperature for at least half an hour. An engine will be wrecked by allowing 'old' oil to remain in it for too long. Valve clearances and chain tension must be checked every 6000 miles (9600 km). Correct chain tension is critical, since a slack chain affects performance.

If you intend to lay up the engine, run it at normal temperature, then drain the oil, renew the filter and fill it with fresh oil. Drain the cooling system, and refill it with fresh antifreeze/water mixture. Run the engine briefly to circulate the oil and water. Remove the spark plugs and pour a little fresh oil down the bores, then turn the engine over by hand. Replace the plugs. Make sure that the engine is kept warm and dry. If possible, periodically remove the plugs, pour more fresh oil down the bores and turn the engine over by hand. Always refit the plugs, otherwise moisture will get in. Engines should last quite a while in this condition—it is moisture getting in through open ports, rusting the valve seats and piston rings to the bores, that ruins an engine. If this does happen, the engine will have to be stripped and rebuilt again.

Overleaf
Rare Elan Sprint and +2S130 brochure

PART THREE

Twin-cam data

1 Engine identification

Head/engine prefixes and camshaft cover recognition

The original colours of the Lotus cam cover denoted the power output and the vehicle application. The cam cover itself underwent three design changes at Lotus.

Up to October 1968, the cover had the word 'Lotus' cast along each side and painted the same colour as the cover itself. The oil cap was circular. From October 1968, the word 'Lotus' was cast in large block capitals at the end of the cover and had a polished-alloy finish, together with its surround. The oil cap was changed to a three-eared type. From October 1970 to the end of production, the cover was ribbed and 'Lotus Big Valve' was cast in place of the word 'Lotus'.

In addition to different cam-cover colours, the engine carried a prefix letter, or letters, to denote its specification and the application for which it had been built. As can be seen from the accompanying table, Lotus produced many varieties, some of which a lot of people do not even realize exist. From 1968 onwards, most of the cylinder heads also carried one of three letters—'H', 'N' or 'S'—stamped on the raised boss at the front of the number one spark-plug well. Again, contrary to information in manuals, books and magazine articles, the stampings have the following meanings:

H   High compression only (10.3:1)
N   High compression and big valves (inlet)
S   Big valves, Federal only, standard compression (9.5:1)

NOTE The latest Lotus workshop manuals (1974, reprint) have amendments to this information. The S/E Stromberg engine is recognized as having a 10.3:1 compression ratio.

Heads built prior to 1968 carried no stamping, and all had a standard 9.5:1 compression ratio and normal valves.

As we have seen, camshafts were:

B-type (standard)	no groove	0.375 in. total lift
C-type (S/E)	one groove	0.3498 in. total lift
D-type (Super S/E, Sprint)	two grooves	0.3600 in. total lift
E-type	plain	0.3659 in. total lift

NOTE Total lift is measured from the base circle. Actual valve lift in the engine is total lift minus the mean cold tappet clearance. For example, with the D-type camshaft, the total lift is 0.3600 in., but the mean inlet-tappet clearance is 0.007 in. and the mean exhaust-tappet clearance is 0.010 in. The actual valve lift, therefore, is 0.3530 in. (inlet) and 0.3500 in. (exhaust).

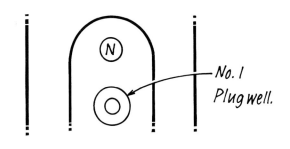

Cylinder-head identification letter in plug well

Camshaft recognition:
No groove indicates standard B-type
One groove indicates S/E C-type
Two grooves indicate Super S/E (Sprint) D-type

1 Twin-cam identification

Serial prefix	Engine type and market	Application and Year	Head stamp	Big Valve	High compression	Camshaft type	Cam-cover colour
C	S/E Weber Domestic and export	Elan 1963 onwards				C	Green
D	Standard Weber Domestic and export	Elan 1963 onwards				B	Dark blue
E	S/E Weber Domestic and export	Lotus-Cortina 1963 onwards				C	Silver (black on Mk II)

Serial prefix	Engine type and market	Application and Year	Head stamp	Big Valve	High compression	Camshaft type	Cam-cover colour
F	S/E Weber Domestic and export	+2 and S 1967				C	Red
G	Stromberg Federal	Elan 1969				C	Red
H	Super S/E Weber Domestic	Elan early 1968	H		√	D	Red
I	Stromberg Federal	+2 1969				C	Red
J	S/E Weber Domestic and export	Escort Twin Cam 1968 onwards				C	Silver early, then black
K	Standard Stromberg Domestic	Elan 1969				C	Black
L	S/E Stromberg Domestic	Elan 1969	H		√	D	Red
M	S/E Stromberg Domestic	+2S 1969	H		√	D	Red
N	Big Valve Weber Domestic	Elan (Sprint) late 1970	N	√	√	D	Black, ribbed
P	Big Valve Weber Domestic	+2S130 late 1970	N	√	√	D	Black, ribbed
Q	S/E Stromberg Domestic	Europa late 1971	H		√	D	Red
R	Big Valve Dellorto Domestic	Europa (Special) late 1972	N	√	√	D	Black, ribbed
S	Big Valve Stromberg Federal	Europa late 1971	S	√		C	Red
T	Big Valve Stromberg Federal	Elan late 1970	S	√		C	Red
U	Big Valve Stromberg Federal	+2S late 1970	S	√		C	Red
V	S/E Dellorto Domestic	Europa very late 1971				C	Red
W	Big Valve Stromberg Federal	Elan late 1970 into 1971	N	√	√	E	Red

Serial prefix	Engine type and market	Application and Year	Head stamp	Big Valve	High compression	Camshaft type	Cam-cover colour
EV	S/E Dellorto European	Europa very late 1971				C	Black
ER	Big Valve Dellorto European	Europa (Special) 1972 onwards	N	√	√	D	Red, ribbed
EN	Big Valve Dellorto European	Elan (Sprint) 1972 onwards	N	√	√	D	Red, ribbed
EP	Big Valve Dellorto European	+2S130 1972 onwards	N	√	√	D	Red, ribbed

Many cam covers are easily swapped; indeed, some of the last domestic-market engines had European (i.e. red) covers, instead of black. The table above gives the original cam-cover colour, as it left the Lotus factory. Other engine tuners, of course, produced their own covers; these are not listed above, as the engine would have been bought from the factory originally.

The colours used were as follows:

Green	BMC (now Austin Rover Group) engine paint as used on A-series engines.	
Blue	Ford rocker-cover paint, as used on Mk I Cortina and related engines.	
Silver	Left polished	
Black	Satin matt black crackle finish	} 'Lotus' and surround left polished.
Red	Poppy red crackle finish	
Black ribbed	Gloss black crackle finish	} 'Lotus Big Valve' and surround
Red ribbed	Signal red crackle finish	and ribs left polished.

The crackle-finish paints are supplied by Trimite Ltd, and must be applied by professional, high-quality stove-enamellers.

NOTE The reds and blacks used are not the same. The gloss black and signal red were carried ovr to the 2 litre and 2.2 litre Type 907, 910, 911 and 912 engines.

The remainder of the engine was painted Lotus Grey—a grey with a touch of blue in it. The nearest equivalent is Massey Ferguson Stoneleigh Grey enamel, to which you should add a little blue enamel.

From a study of the engine-identification table, it comes as a surprise to see that Lotus made 24 varieties of the twin-cam. Many of these require quantifying. After the production of the engine became standardized at Hethel, from 1967 onwards, the official power figures (shown right) can be taken as representative across the whole spectrum; after all, the build and test procedures were the same for all engines.

Engine	Gross bhp	@ rpm
Standard Weber/Stromberg	103–105	5500
S/E Weber	112–115	6000
S/E Stromberg	115–118	6000
Big Valve Weber/Dellorto	125–126	6500
Federal Stromberg	(108)	6500
Federal Big Valve Stromberg	(110)	6500
European Big Valve Dellorto	121–122	6500

Maximum torque

Engine	lb ft	@ rpm
1498 cc	102	4500
1558 cc standard	108	4000
S/E	108	4000
Big Valve	113	5500
Big Valve emission	104	5000

It must be stressed that no domestic engine ever gave less than 103 bhp, despite many historians quoting 93 bhp or so. This arises from another mistake in the 1974 reprint of the workshop manuals, which listed the standard engine at 93 bhp. The original 1498 cc engine gave 98–100 bhp.

The major revelation is that the high-compression head (10.3:1) was in existence a full two years before the Big Valve announcement. This is why, with the D-type cams fitted, the domestic Stromberg engine goes very quickly indeed, and gives rise to the 3 bhp discrepancy compared to the 115 bhp of the Weber S/E. The standard Stromberg engine retained the normal head but had C-type cams to restore peak power to the 103–105 bhp of the standard Weber engine. All the workshop manuals and handbooks quote the standard compression of 9.5:1 for the S/E, which is wrong; this should be amended to 10.3:1. This fact alone explains why owners of domestic S/Es experience major pinking problems when running on RM-rating four-star fuel of 97–99 octane. Standard engines of 9.5:1 run happily on 97–99 octane. All high-compression engines required 101 octane, but since the demise of this fuel the Stromberg-engined cars suffer most, as they run leaner than the Weber/Dellorto engines. The problem increases if the head is skimmed further.

All Stromberg-engined +2Ss and Europas (prefix M and Q) were S/E type with up to 118 bhp. No standard Stromberg engines were fitted to these cars; only the Elan (prefix K) had this engine, as it was far lighter in weight than the other two cars. Prefix Q, the Stromberg S/E engine for the Europa, is an odd variant and very few ever left the factory. The reason for the initial batch of twin-cam Europas being on Strombergs, after production of the Renault-powered Europa ended, was that due to the government pollution specification 1501 of 1970–71, the factory realized that Weber carburettors would fail the pollution-test procedures (which, indeed, they did), and as an interim measure, before the running change to Dellortos was made, the Strombergs were used. It was not because Lotus had run out of Webers! (Prefixes N and P were initially on Webers, but kept the same prefix letter when Dellortos were fitted.)

One questions the launch of the twin-cam Europa in late 1971, since the official power output was given as 105 bhp, and great play was made about the stresses imposed upon the Renault 336 gearbox (the original reason, of course, why the twin-cam was not introduced earlier was that the gearbox was the weak link). However, the first twin-cam Europas had the 336 gearbox, albeit to Federal specification, but some domestic ones appeared, so with the Europa actually having 115 + bhp instead of the claimed 105 bhp (prefixes Q, V and EV), it is no wonder the 336 gearbox tended to expire extremely quickly. Only when the stronger Type 352 gearbox came into production was the problem solved. Officially, no Europa engine ever appeared with Webers; Dellortos were used solely because of the emission problem, and the Europa came after the Big Valve Elan and +2S130.

Grave doubts exist as to the actual power outputs of the Federal engines with Strombergs. Officially, these produced 108/110 bhp, but on analysis the engines could only give 97–98 bhp, which would give credence to the large number of complaints about the cars being under-powered, with poor acceleration and generally diabolical performance (prefixes G, I, S, T and U). The G and I versions had C-type cams—not the D-type of the domestic S/E—and in this specification alone, on the domestic market, would give 103–105 bhp as prefix K. The Federal engines did not have high compression (this was outlawed) and, with the emission equipment, the power would drop further by at least 5 bhp. As we have already seen, the Big Valve version (S, T and U) would only produce an extra 1 bhp, so that total output was still below 100 bhp. One can only assume that the factory was embarrassed about dropping below the magical 100 bhp figure, or that Federal sales would have been severely curtailed if the true figure had been given. Possibly because of this, the odd engine was produced (prefix W), which had a different camshaft from any other twin-cam made.

Until this book was written, no one, outside key factory personnel, ever knew that a fourth camshaft was used. The E-type cam profile was originally drawn by Dennis Brown for the 'new' Jensen Healey engine, the 2 litre 907. This cam gave far better torque characteristics than the D-type, but with the same power output, which tended to 'come in' immediately. This was not too much of a problem in the Stromberg Big Valves because of the nature of the twin-cam engine and the weight of the cars. However, when placed in the Jensen Healey and later the Elites (type 75), the cars gave rise to poor low-down torque.

A Stromberg-carburetted engine for an Elan S4, showing the high-level balance pipe. The air box is a one-piece item on all Stromberg models, but there is a metal backplate and GRP air box, for Weber and Dellorto-carburetted engines

The D-type cam raised the maximum torque, over the standard and S/E engines, to 5500 rpm, which is only 1000 rpm down from maximum power. The E-type cam profile was then used on a development twin-cam engine and, with big valves and high compression on Strombergs, was found to give better torque characteristics and hence performance, generating around 110 bhp (prefix L gave 115–118 bhp). The factory are unaware of any of these engines being released, but what a prospect—if the E-type was placed in the domestic Big Valve, there would be a sensational torque band across a much lower and wider rpm range.

Prefixes ER, EN and EP were really the same as domestic engines, but had different carburettor jets (see table) and ignition settings to meet the European specification. Up to 1968, this was the same as for the domestic market—in fact, those early engines were sold everywhere! Federal is not the same as later European specification, Federal is USA specification.

Prefix H is also very rare, being the Super S/E Weber (see text) which gave 124–125 bhp a full two years before the Big Valve appeared. As we have seen, the big valve gives 1 bhp over standard. The 0.040 in.-skimmed head and Weber carburettors account for approximately 6 bhp compared with the Stromberg S/E. The fabricated four-branch manifold, compared with the cast-iron version, gave 3–4 bhp more. The maximum bhp ever seen at Hethel was 128 bhp from a Big Valve engine with Webers.

2 Specifications

Carburation specifications

These tables cover all Lotus production specifications, and some have not been published before, namely the small-valve Dellorto settings. Weber and Dellorto carburettors are completely interchangeable, the only necessary alterations being to the choke linkage and fuel lines.

Weber carburettors
Type 40 DCOE 18 used on early standard and S/E engines
Type 40 DCOE 31 used on late standard S/E and Big Valve engines
All settings are identical for type 18 and 31, unless stated otherwise

	Standard (B-type cam)	S/E (C-type cam)	Super S/E and Big Valve (D-type cam)
Choke	30 mm	32 mm	33 mm
Main jet	115	115	120
Air-corrector jet	200	150	155
Slow-running jet	50F8 (45F9 type 18)	50F8	50F8
Accelerator-pump jet	40	40	35
Accelerator-pump stroke	10 mm	10 mm	10 mm
Starter air jet	100	100	100
Starter petrol jet	F.5/100	F.5/100	F.5/100
Emulsion tube	F11	F11	F11
Needle valve	1.75	1.75	1.75
Air-trumpet (ram pipe) length	1.50 in./3.8 cm (1.75 in./4.4 cm type 18)	1.5 in./3.8 cm	1.5 in./3.8 cm
Float levels	8.5 and 15 mm	8.5 and 15 mm	8.5 and 15 mm
Idle speed	800–900 rpm	800–900 rpm	900–950 rpm

On some S/E engines a flat spot occurred around 2000 rpm and, at the time, Lotus recommended that this could be overcome in one of two ways: by fitting a large accelerator-pump jet (35 instead of 40), which would increase fuel consumption, or by fitting 30-mm chokes instead of the 32 mm versions, together with a 200 air-corrector jet instead of a 150. The latter would be more satisfactory, but top-end power would be slightly reduced, by approximately 3 bhp over 5000 rpm.

The Type 40 DCOE 31, as jetted for the Big Valve specification, will cope easily up to a tune of 140 bhp. There is no need to rejet for a road-specification engine.

Float levels are measured from the cover (with gasket fitted) to the top of the float and are adjusted by bending the respective tags.

Dellorto carburettors

Type DHLA 40 used on all domestic small-valve and Big Valve engines
Type DHLA 40E used on all European ECE 15 engines
NOTE Some of the last Big Valve engines for the domestic market also had the European-specification carburettor, presumably correctly jetted.

	Domestic S/E small valve (C-type cam)	European S/E (C-type cam)	Domestic Big Valve (D-type cam)	European Big Valve (D-type cam)
Colour code (original)	green	green	red	red
Choke	30	30	33	32
Main jet	115	120	120	120
Air-corrector jet	160	200	130	160
Slow-running jet	50	45L	50	50L
Idle-jet holder	7850-2	7850-4	7850-2	7850-1
Emulsion tube	7772-1	7772-5	7772-5	7772-5
Pump jet	40	33	35	33
Starter jet	70	70	70	70
Starter emulsion tube	7482-1	7482-1	7482-1	7482-1
Needle valve	150	150	150	150
Air-trumpet (ram pipe) length	40 cm	40 cm	40 cm	40 cm
Float levels	14.5–15.0 mm*	16.5–17.0 mm	14.5–15.0 mm*	16.5–17.0 mm
Idle speed	900–950 rpm	900–950 rpm	900–950 rpm	900–950 rpm

*If there is persistent flooding, set the float levels to the European specification.

Type DHLA 40 jetted for domestic Big Valve will easily cope with up to 140 bhp for road conditions—no change is required. Float levels are measured with the gasket fitted.

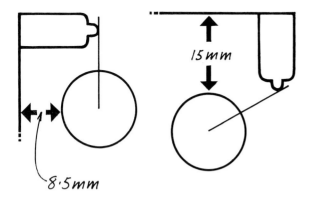

Weber carburettor float height

Stromberg carburettors

Type 175 CD2S used for domestic (non-emission) engines
Type 175 CD2SE used for emission engines only

	CD2S (C/D-type cam)	CD2SE (C/D-type cam)
Needle	BIY (later 2 BAR, floating)*	BIG
Spring colour	Natural	Blue/black
Damper oil	20W-50 engine oil (not synthetic)	20W-50 engine oil (not synthetic)
Float level	16–17 mm	16–17 mm
Idle speed	800–900 rpm	950 rpm

*See Running-in section.

If a small-valve engine is rebuilt to Big Valve specifications, there is no need to change the needle settings.

The Stromberg carburettors used were made by Zenith, with temperature compensators and settings designed specifically to meet the twin-cam engine's requirements. Stromberg 175-size carburettors fitted to Volvos, Vauxhalls and other makes are not interchangeable.

NOTE The factory offer this advice for twin-cam engined cars used in North America, where they are operated principally at altitudes above 4000 feet (1219 metres).

On all North American-specification Elans, +2s and Europa T/Cs built from 1968 onwards:

1 Replace Stromberg carburettor metering needle assembly BIG by needle assembly BIGA. Adjust the engine idle as specified.
2 Fit the Lotus label A036U1267 adjacent to the Emission Control Information label.

Tightening torques

	lb ft	kg m		lb ft	kg m
Cylinder head (cold)	60–65	8.29–8.98	Water-pump pulley/fan		
Cylinder head/front cover	15	2.07	assembly	8	1.10
Spark plugs	25	3.45	Timing-chain tensioner		
Cam cover	6–8	0.83–1.10	sprocket pin	40–45	5.53–6.22
Camshaft bearing caps	9	1.24	retaining bolt	45–50	6.22–6.91
Camshaft sprockets	25	3.45	pivot pin	40–45	5.53–6.22
Crankshaft bearing caps			Jackshaft		
all four- and six-bolt	55–60	7.60–8.29	sprocket	12–15	1.65–2.07
Connecting rod caps			retaining plate	5–7	0.69–0.96
C-type	44–46	6.08–6.36	Oil-gallery plugs	8	1.10
L-type	25	3.45	Sump	8	1.10
Crankshaft pulley	25	3.45	Sump drain plug	20–25	2.76–3.45
Flywheel			Oil pump		
all four- and six-bolt	45	6.22	Fuel pump		
Clutch cover	18–20	2.48–2.76	Rear oil-seal housing		
Front cover			four- and six-bolt	15–18	2.07–2.48
all ¼ in. bolts	5–7	0.69–0.96	Engine mountings and/or		
$\frac{5}{16}$ in. bolt	10–15	1.38–2.07	brackets		
Backplate to cylinder			Exhaust manifolds		
block	6–8	0.83–1.10	all types		

	lb ft	kg m			lb ft	kg m
Dynamo/alternator bracket to cylinder block	20	2.76		Weber/Dellorto air box ($\frac{1}{4}$ in. UNF)	8	1.10
Weber/Dellorto trumpet nuts (6 mm)	8	1.10		Stromberg air box ($\frac{5}{16}$ in. UNC)	12–15	1.65–2.07
Weber/Dellorto fuel banjo bolt	16	2.21		Oil-filter centre bolt (renewable paper element		
Weber (early) air box ($\frac{5}{16}$ in. UNC)	12–15	1.65–2.07		only)	12–15	1.65–2.07

Specifications, fits and clearances

Engine

Bore	3.250 in. (82.550 mm)
Stroke	2.864 in. (72.746 mm)
Capacity	95.06 cu.in. (1558 cc)
Compression ratio	9.5:1
	10.3:1 (Big Valve)
Compression pressure (hot)	
9.5:1	In excess of 160 psi (11.248 kg/sq.cm)
10.3:1	In excess of 170 psi (11.950 kg/sq.cm)

All to be within 20 psi (1.406 kg sq cm) of each other

Firing order	1-3-4-2
Normal oil pressure (hot)	35–40 psi (2.4–2.8 kg/sq.cm)

Cylinder head

Material	Aluminium alloy, LM8 WP, die-cast or sand-cast, heated to 535-540 degrees Celsius for five to seven hours and quenched in hot water. Reheated to 110–130 degrees Celsius for five hours, air cooled, then machined. No further treatment required
Inclination of valves	27 degrees from vertical (54 degrees included angle)
Combustion chambers	Fully machined, hemispherical
Head-gasket material	Copper/asbestos (treated with Shellac on both sides)
Valve-guide material	Cast-iron
Valve-insert (seat) material	Cast-iron
Valve-insert and face angle	45 degrees
Inlet-valve material (small-valve and Big Valve)	Silicon chromium valve steel EN52, tip hard, chrome-plated and flame-hardened to Rockwell C48-52
Exhaust-valve material (current)	Valve steel 21.4NS, no chrome or heat treatment
Valve-head diameter	
Inlet	1.526–1.530 in. (38.760–38.862 mm)
Big Valve inlet	1.560–1.566 in. (39.776 mm)
Exhaust	1.321–1.325 in. (33.553–33.655 mm)
Valve-stem diameter	0.310–0.311 in. (7.874–7.899 mm)
Cylinder-head bore for guides (std)	0.499–0.4995 in. (12.674–12.687 mm)

Oversize guides available at 0.001, 0.005 and 0.006 in.

Cylinder-head bore for inserts (std)
    Inlet   1.6235–1.6245 in. (41.237–41.252 mm)
    Exhaust   1.4985–1.4995 in. (38.062–38.087 mm)
    Oversize inserts available at 0.005, 0.010 and 0.015 in.
Valve stem to guide clearance
    Inlet   0.0003–0.0023 in. (0.007–0.058 mm)
    Exhaust   0.0025–0.0030 in. (0.063–0.076 mm)
Valve clearances (cold)
    Inlet   0.005–0.007 in. (0.127–0.177 mm)
    Exhaust   0.009–0.011 in. (0.228–0.279 mm)
Tappet (cam follower) material   Chilled, close-grained cast-iron (oil finished)
Tappet outside diameter   1.3742–1.3745 in. (34.903–34.911 mm)
Tappet running clearance to sleeve   0.0005–0.0014 in. (0.013–0.036 mm)
Camshaft material   Monikrom high-duty cast-iron, chilled on cam lobes. Camshafts running in steel-backed, white-metal bearings. No oversize available
Camshaft journal diameter   1.000–1.0005 in. (25.400–25.413 mm)
Camshaft running clearance (journal to bearing)   0.0005–0.002 in. (0.013–0.051 mm)
Camshaft endfloat   0.003–0.010 in. (0.076–0.254 mm)
Line-bore in head   1.125–1.126 in.
Valve-spring material   Steel wire (EN49) peened to a depth of 0.014 ±0.002 in. and oiled. Made to an original Lotus drawing in Germany

Valve-spring free length
    Inner   1.130 in. (28.70 mm)
    Outer   1.450 in. (36.83 mm)
Outer valve-spring load
    @ 1.17 in. (29.718 mm)   45 lb (20.4 kg)
    @ 0.83 in. (21.082 mm)   109 lb (49.4 kg)
Inner valve-spring load
    @ 0.92 in. (23.368 mm)   12.4 lb (5.6 kg)
    @ 0.58 in. (14.732 mm)   33.5 lb (15.2 kg)
Valve-spring retainer   Made to an original Lotus drawing in EN16T steel, as are the collets and spring seats
Front-cover material   LM4M die-cast aluminium
Water pump   Lotus own-design impellor, housing and O-rings; Ford bearing, seal and hub
Running clearance (impellor/housing)   0.025–0.030 in. (0.635–0.800 mm)

Cylinder block
Material   Ford cast-iron with full-length water jackets. Graded blocks, and originally graded bore size (1–4) to match graded A- and C-type pistons (1–4)
Line-bore (block/main caps)   2.2710–2.2715 in. (57.683–57.696 mm)
Jackshaft material   Ford cast-iron, running in three steel-backed, white-metal bearings
Jackshaft journal diameter   1.560–1.5605 in. (39.624–39.637 mm)
Jackshaft endfloat   0.0025–0.0075 in. (0.063–0.190 mm)
Jackshaft bearing length
    Front and rear   0.75 in. (19.05 mm)
    Centre   0.64 in. (16.26 mm)
    Oversize available only on OD standard ID
Jackshaft running clearance   0.001–0.002 in. (0.025–0.050 mm)

Crankshaft

Material	Ford nodular graphite cast-iron, high-strength EM-1A-4. Oilways tested to 75–80 psi. Bearings—steel-backed, lead bronze with lead indium overlay. Original drawings made in 1962
Main journals	2.1255–2.1260 in. (53.987–54.000 mm)
Big-end journals	1.9370–1.9375 in. (49.199–49.211 mm)
Endfloat	0.003–0.011 in. (0.076–0.279 mm)
Running clearance on bearing	0.0015–0.003 in. (0.038–0.076 mm)
Maximum undersize for regrind	0.03 in. (0.762 mm)

Connecting rod

Material	H-section forged steel, steel-backed, lead-bronze bearings with lead indium overlay. Small-end bush—steel-backed bronze
Running clearance	
Big-end bearing	0.0005–0.0022 in. (0.013–0.513 mm)
Small-end to gudgeon pin	0.0003–0.0005 in. (0.008–0.13 mm)
Endfloat on crankpin	0.004–0.010 in. (0.101–0.254 mm)
Length between centres	4.799–4.801 in. (121.899–121.945 mm)

Pistons

Solid-skirt, tin-plated aluminium alloy, with fully-floating, machined, seamless-steel-tube gudgeon pins, held in by circlips. Pistons were originally graded in production to blocks, the grading being 1–4 in 0.0003-in. (0.008-mm) steps. Grading is now obsolete with no new blocks and 'one-size' pistons. A rebore destroys the grading immediately. Grading was for production purposes only. Any standard or 0.015 in. (0.38 mm) Lotus pistons left are C-type, i.e. with small cut-outs. All Powermax pistons have large cut-outs, like the original A-type. However, they are not the same material as the A-type. The original grading was for standard pistons only.

A-type and C-type pistons. Note that A-types have larger cut-outs

A-type grading range (1–4)	3.2470–3.2473 to 3.2479–3.2482 in. (82.466–82.474 to 82.489–82.497 mm)
C-type grading range (1–4)	3.2467–3.2470 to 3.2476–3.2479 in. (82.466–82.474 to 82.489–82.490 mm)
Length	2.687 in. (68.25 mm)
Compression height	1.536–1.538 in. (39.014–39.065 mm)
Piston rings	2 compression (equal size A-type only); 1 oil control
Clearance in block bore	
A-type	0.0027–0.0033 in. (0.068–0.083 mm)
C-type (std and 0.015 in.)	0.0030–0.0036 in. (0.076–0.091 mm)
Powermax (std, 0.020, 0.030 and 0.040 in.)	0.0029–0.0032 in. (0.074–0.081 mm)
Gudgeon-pin/piston sliding fit	0–0.0002 in. (0–0.0051 mm)
Piston-ring gap in bore	
Compression	0.009–0.014 in. (0.229–0.356 mm)
Oil control	0.010–0.020 in. (0.254–0.508 mm)
Piston-ring to groove	
Compression	0.0016–0.0036 in. (0.041–0.091 mm)
Oil control	0.0018–0.0038 in. (0.046–0.097 mm)

Rings are cast-iron and chrome-plated (some top), copper-plated for identification purposes (A- and C-type). Powermax rings come in sets of four for all standard to 0.040 in. pistons

Flywheel

Maximum run-out	0.004 in. (0.101 mm)
Run-out on ring gear	
Lateral	0.016 in. (0.406 mm)
Radial	0.006 in. (0.152 mm)
Number of teeth	110
Spigot bearing	
Four-bolt crankshaft	Sintered bronze bush
Six-bolt crankshaft	Needle-roller type

Timing chain

Type	Single roller
Pitch	0.375 in. (9.525 mm)
Length in pitches	120
Roller diameter	0.250 in. (6.350 mm)
Roller width	0.225 in. (5.615 mm)
Breaking load	2000 lb (910 kg)

3 What to look for

Looking at a Lotus twin-cam engined car for the first time can be a little daunting, unless you know what to expect. The following is provided as a guide:

Oil leaks

These engines do not leak oil when properly built; new ones from the factory never leaked. However, on an old engine, oil may be pouring out everywhere, so check to see if a high-pressure oil pump is fitted, which runs at 55–60 psi hot, instead of 38–40 psi. The backplate/front cover on the block may be distorted, and is a potential source of a major oil leak. Oil leaking from cam D-plugs and the top of the cam cover may be due to a lack of Senloc washers. Check the front and rear oil seals (unfortunately, due to design, four-bolt-crank engines will leak from their cork or asbestos rear seals after about 20,000 miles).Oil may leak out of the fuel-pump lubrication bleed hole (it dribbles over the starter motor)—a strip-down and new gasket is the only cure.

Water pump

Rock the hub—if it is very loose, a pump overhaul is required. On starting the engine, check that the pump does not screech or rumble. Make sure that no water leaks from the bleed hole in the front cover. The water pump does not give trouble when it is correctly installed.

Running

On starting up, the engine should turn over easily. If it clanks into life, the starter ring gear and/or Bendix drive may be smashed. When hot, there should be no undue clanking noises. A bottom-end clank from cold, which disappears when hot, indicates worn out big-end bearings and/or piston slap. A light tapping noise from the top end is

normal, but if it is excessive, becoming less obvious when hot, this indicates worn tappets in their sleeves. A pronounced tap could indicate a very worn tappet on its own, or a cam-lobe problem, or an excessive valve clearance.

When driving the car, if there is a blue haze from the exhaust on acceleration, the piston rings are very worn; if a blue haze appears on deceleration, it is worn valve guides. If the water-temperature gauge rises with increased engine speed, then falls back at low rpm, it is usually an indication of a blown head gasket. In this situation, the cooling system is being pressurized, with subsequent water loss. Upon idle, white exhaust 'smoke' may also be seen—this is water vapour. Falling or flickering oil pressure at speed usually indicates badly-worn main and big-end bearings or, possibly, but rarely, a faulty oil pump.

When the engine is hot, a compression test will also reveal its condition; if all cylinders are within 20 lb of each other, but the pressures overall are low, this indicates a good engine with clearances becoming a little worn. A low reading (or even zero) from one cylinder would indicate a blown head gasket, a burnt valve and/or broken piston rings. A burnt valve also gives a regular 'whooshing' beat like a blowing exhaust pipe.

After a test run, make sure the head gasket is not 'sizzling' between head and block with oil or water bubbling out. These engines never weep at this gasket; do not believe stories that they did. Check also the length of timing-chain adjuster which is left—if there is very little, the chain is badly worn. A loose chain may rattle, and if really loose, it will hit the top of the cam cover. A chain that is too tight will 'scream' as the revs increase.

In standard form—that means with standard

cam profiles—all twin-cam engines idle evenly and run smoothly and progressively throughout the rev range. Check that any rough running is not attributable to maladjusted or out-of-balance carburation, and that 'kick-in-the-pants' power at around 5000 rpm is not due to a peaky camshaft or specially-jetted carbs.

An engine can always be viewed in two ways; all the foregoing is irrelevant if the engine is to be rebuilt, but it should be taken seriously if the car being sold is in good or bad order generally. If the seller claims that the engine has been rebuilt and the purchase is accepted, it will come as a rude shock if it disintegrates a few miles later. Always seek professional guidance—it is far better to be safe than sorry.

4 Exploding the myths

There is no such thing as a Mk I or a Mk II twin-cam. Engines up to number 7799, with the four-bolt crankshaft, were known as 'rope-seal' engines. After that, the six-bolt version was known as the 'lip-seal' engine, on account of its rear oil-seal arrangement.

There is no such thing as an early or a late head—the 'early' heads are die-cast and the 'late' heads are sand-cast. Die-cast heads have 'half-moon' protrusions in the plug wells.

Head gaskets do not weep when the engine is running. Nobody has ever seen a new weeping twin-cam engine.

Heads are not porous—one or two sub-standard heads, produced outside Lotus for certain people, may have been porous, and the myth grew. However, no warranty claims exist to substantiate the rumours. Heads may be 'porous' now, after years of abuse, but most so-called porosity is due to internal cracks caused by a total lack of care.

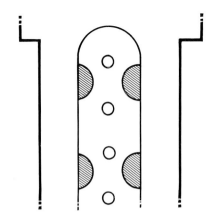

Die-cast heads have half-moon protusions in the plug wells

Twin-cam engines do not pour out oil; if built correctly, as outlined in this book, they will not leak. They leak only because owners refuse to pay money for the correct gaskets, sealants and washers, and because amateurs rebuild them.

Water pumps do not fail persistently—in fact, correctly installed, the pump gives very little trouble. When new, the cars were typically doing 10–12,000 miles a year, and the pumps lasted for five years at least. Now, with limited use, the engine being thrashed in summer and laying idle all winter, it is little wonder that the pump fails more often (this applies to all components, of course). The V-belt must not be over-tightened, as this will impose a side load on the pump bearing, which is a reason why, with the fixed-length, non-adjustable V-belt on the Europa, its pump lasts three to four times as long as the others. This fact alone bears out the customer-induced complaints about Elan and +2 water pumps. At that time, Lotus warranty personnel, Colin Fish and Mike Pomfret, had to educate customers and dealers alike on how to tighten the V-belt. They never had any complaints about Europa pumps, other than material and component failures. Unfortunately, many small firms have cashed in on this 'fault' and produce bolt-on pumps and different pulley/cogged-belt arrangements, in an attempt to reduce the side load. Some of these kits are good, but some are very bad. Often, the result is that after the customer has paid the high cost of the new front cover and pump, the bolt-on pump fails far sooner than the original ever would.

(It is ironic that Lotus only ever had two warranty 'problems'. One, already mentioned, was not really a problem; the other was of high oil consumption. Once again, the customer had to be re-educated—that a high-performance engine uses more oil than a sedate unit. In Mike Pomfret's words, 'The twin-cam was one of the most reliable things we've ever done; warranty claims were negligible over its whole run'. Indeed, he could not remember ever having any head or block failures; the only failures were of the material kind, such as valve springs breaking in half.)

Road engines do not require a high-pressure oil pump. Actually, more harm is done by blasting oil across the bearing surface, since it does not offer its correct lubrication and cooling properties. The normal oil pressure is 35–40 psi, not 65–70 psi. Indeed, as Tony Rudd points out, the twin-cam crankshaft requires a minimum of 45 psi oil pressure to provide it with total lubrication up to 7000 rpm. Race engines require high pressure because of their higher rev limits. However, on road engines, a high-pressure oil pump will only serve to blow oil from every gasket—which gives rise to the myth that all Lotus twin-cam engines leak. Do not refit a high-pressure oil pump when rebuilding an engine. Similarly, engine oil coolers are not needed unless the car is to be used in ambient temperatures above 40 degrees Celsius. If an oil cooler is to be fitted, use a thermostatically-controlled item. Usually, more harm is caused by the engine oil being too cold, for this causes increased wear and sludging.

The twin-cam engine does not 'eat' starter rings. Lotus never deviated from using a 110-tooth ring gear and a nine-tooth Bendix gear. This arrangement was common to all twin-cam engines built between 1962 and 1975. (A lot of nonsense has been spoken, and written, on this subject by private rebuilders—do not fit anything else.) The only reason for the starting system breaking down is because the starter-motor locating plate (backplate) may be broken on Elan and +2 models, which allows the starter motor to move, wrecking the gear and Bendix drive. On the five-speed +2, the problem is magnified because of its alloy bellhousing; the threads become stripped, with devastating results. If the plate has become broken or distorted, discard it in favour of a replacement—do not weld-up the old one. Fit a new ring gear (the right way round), together with a new starter motor, and there should never be any trouble again. On five-speed cars, Helicoil the bellhousing ($\frac{3}{8}$ in. UNC) to accept two new fixing bolts.

NOTE As part of its rationalization programme, Lucas discontinued its nine-tooth-pinion starter-motor Bendix in favour of a ten-tooth pinion during 1986–87. All new starter motors supplied for twin-cams from early 1987 had ten-tooth Bendix pinions.

(The author's own Elan is now 17 years old, and has completed more than 100,000 miles—it is still fitted with the original ring gear and starter motor and, incidentally, is only on its second water pump. . . .)

5 Parts situation

Lotus are keen to maintain the supply of parts for the twin-cam engine, as it is a much-needed source of revenue for them. They need not have undertaken this commitment, for the usual 'ten-year' manufacturers' rule (whereby major car manufacturers honour a ten-year unofficial guarantee of parts supply after any particular model has been dropped) has long since elapsed. However, in 1976, a directive from Michael Kimberley to remove all extraneous early Elan and Europa parts, culminating in 1979 with a possibility of all twin-cam-era parts being hived off in order to gain much needed space for 2 litre production and other commitments, coupled with declining sales of twin-cam car parts, made the future look grim. In 1974 Roy Smith, the chief buyer, undertook the task of securing an all-time requirement (ATR) across the twin-cam vehicle range; it is to his great credit that this ATR lasted into 1984 and 1985, i.e. ten years. Until recently, Lotus themselves were, unaware of the continuing need for parts for their early cars due to the growing classic-car movement. In the void created by this lack of awareness, many 'instant' specialists appeared—some good, but some very bad indeed—to take business away from Lotus and its dealers. The Sevens are looked after by Caterham Car Sales, and the remaining stock of factory Lotus-Cortina (Type 28) parts went there as well. In 1977 the original Elite model (Type 14) was given to the author at Fibreglass Services.

Fortunately, through the realization of what was happening, and after pressure from certain of its dealers, the Lotus factory (mainly through Hugh Wilson and Roy Smith) set about resourcing and maintaining a permanent supply of parts, to continue for an indefinite period. In 1986, the turnover of twin-cam vehicle and engine parts accounted for £1.5 million. Lotus will be reluctant to lose that kind of revenue unless, of course, its owners, General Motors, decree otherwise. (GM acquired Lotus for £22.7 million in January 1986). At the time of writing, the GM policy towards Lotus is that all will continue as it has been, but that Lotus must stand on its own feet. It is hoped that Lotus will continue to supply its dealers for as long as the marque remains extant, in order that the correct-specification parts remain available. This is critically important in trying to combat some of the specialists who offer cheap alternatives. Lotus, through its legal departments, has set about trying to protect its own interests, but many see this step as coming too late.

The main parts difficulties include the fact that the blocks will not be produced again by Ford. The last genuine block was sold from the Lotus factory in 1979. Crankshafts are no longer produced, although in 1975 Lotus looked at the possibility of producing a replacement, and Graham Atkin produced a drawing based on a Ford 1500 crankshaft with extra screwed-on counter-balance weights. The project did not come to fruition. Specialist firms—principally Gordon Allen—produce new twin-cam cranks for both road and race, and C-type rods are still produced by Ford for Lotus. The factory only ever kept standard and 0.0015 in. oversize pistons, and stocks are now well down. However, Hepolite produce the full range of Powermax pistons from standard through to 0.040 in. oversize. All main, big-end, camshaft, small-end and jackshaft bearings are available, as are all the head and valve-gear parts.

In 1985 Lotus reintroduced the front timing cover in slightly strengthened form. The reintroduction of the backplate (which has been unavailable for several years) is promised soon. The water pump is always available, as are the gasket sets. Ford introduced an improved water-pump seal in late 1984 (Lotus approved) that does away with the brass slinger, and this has been in current supply from early 1985. The front and rear oil seals, also made by Ford, underwent a material change during 1985–86 that allowed them to slide out on their own; fortunately, the material was changed back to the original specification. At present, the cam cover is available in Big Valve form, but there is now no likelihood of the other types being made. All studs and bolts are available. Fuel pump, oil pump and pipes, jackshaft and engine mounting will all continue.

Distributors have gone out of stock, but, due to the demand, Lotus and Lucas have introduced a new distributor which replaces the original 41189 and 41225 types.

Dellorto carburettors are readily available, as are Webers (although, at the time of writing, the 40 DCOE dies are being remade by Weber). The Solex/Zenith group was liquidated in 1985. The result is that Burlen Fuel Systems, of Salisbury, Wiltshire, are now distributors of genuine parts with full manufacturing rights to the original Solex/Zenith UK specifications. If the demand eventually warrants it, Burlen will manufacture a production run of the twin-cam Stromberg 175 CD2S carburettor. However, the emission-type 175 CD2SE will never be reintroduced. Also, 2 BAR needles can be produced if the demand is high enough (at present, no 2 BAR needles exist). Through Burlen Fuel Systems, all gaskets, jets, diaphragms and temperature compensators are available and will be kept in stock indefinitely.

Lotus produce the backplates (these were reintroduced in 1985), air boxes and trunking for all the different carburettors. The original AC Delco air-filter canister went out of stock in 1984, but is currently being produced in its original form by Fibreglass Services.

Camshafts are available from various sources, but there will always be firms who will undertake reprofiling to any specification. However, Lotus have always supplied the D-type (Sprint) camshaft, and in 1985 resourced an update on the original specification (Monikrom high-duty cast-iron, chilled on the cam lobes). Standard and S/E (B- and C-type) cams are out of stock at present. Flywheels are current, as is the ring gear (Ford).

Lotus themselves have to rely on subcontractors for the parts they do not make themselves, and sometimes this leads to delays when components are not delivered on time. Many parts have to be ordered in small batch quantities (Lotus do not enjoy big-manufacturer status, like Jaguar, where batches may mean tens of thousands), and this leads to a problem of pricing. If a batch lasts many years and the price structure is not altered year by year, anomalies arise when the next batch is delivered and priced—an example was the cylinder-head bolt, which went from 93p to £4.75 in one leap. Periodically, Lotus suffered from lack of finances, and Roy Smith admits that his hands were tied, since his parts-budget directive allowed him to spend only so much per month. Most important were current production parts, so at certain times to resource 'old' spares seemed impossible. This was another reason why lengthy delays in the supply of twin-cam parts occurred during the late 1970s and early 1980s. With the easing of the financial situation in 1983—under David Wickens, and now GM—the parts budget may go back to where it should be.

One final problem that occurs from time to time is a communications breakdown between dealers, factory and subcontractor. Fortunately, this is rare, but at present—and this has been unresolved for the last three years—is the case of the composition of the timing-chain damper rubber; it is too soft. The subcontractor has changed his rubber mix, the dealer finds they 'melt' after a year in use, when the oil attacks the rubber to form a soft, almost jelly-like pad. The original specification allowed the rubber to go very hard in continuous use. Dealers report back to Lotus who, in turn, report back to the subcontractor, but after three years nothing has been done yet.

The last twin-cam headache, that has seemingly been going on for ever, is the reintroduction of Weber-carburettor heads. The last official Weber head was sold in 1976, but a few Stromberg heads are still available. Lotus, possibly through pressures of car production, outside engineering contracts or even lack of extra finance, have never really considered producing spare heads. Perhaps they thought the demand was not there. Even so, with all their in-house machining capability for the modern 2 litre and 2.2 litre engines, Lotus could easily machine and finish the twin-cam head for sale, complete with guides, seats, tappet

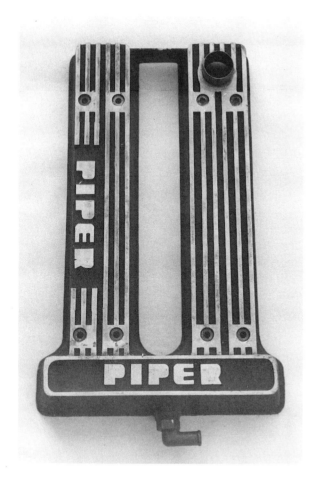
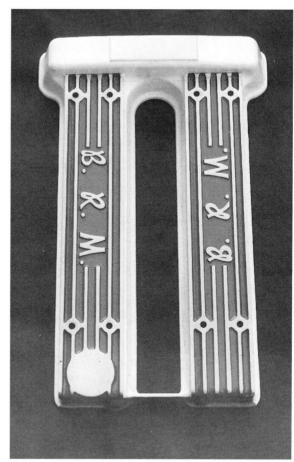

Two versions of the special cam-cover theme. The BRM cover is highly prized today

inserts and studs. Yet, as each year goes by, the demand increases steadily and, of course, many old heads are no longer salvageable.

Graham Nearn, of Caterham Car Sales, who has been involved with the twin-cam (Weber) head through most of its problems, approached Lotus during 1984 with a request for the remanufacture of cylinder heads. He and Martin Long came to an agreement which resulted in a contract being drawn up. This contract, however, was not signed for many months.

In the meantime, David Wakefield, also of Caterham Car Sales, persuaded Barron-Clark of Peterborough to cast two heads from the original, albeit touched-up, pattern equipment. The first suffered from variable wall thickness, and the second was only accepted with reluctance. Although Cosworth Engineering had originally expressed an interest in tackling the machining,

everyone—Mike Costin, Tony Rudd and Martin Long—who saw the castings was horrified. It was 1962/1963 all over again! Obviously, the old pattern equipment was worn out, so in June 1985 David and Barron-Clark looked into the cost of producing new patterns, which proved to be approximately £12,000.

In the light of this, and coupled with the promise of substantial royalties being available to Lotus, Graham Nearn negotiated a change to the original contract. This was approved by Lotus' company secretary, Tom Monk, but was still not approved by managing director Mike Kimberley. Later Mike discussed the matter with Graham Nearn, but requested that availability in Canada and the USA should be excluded from the supply agreements (for product-liability reasons). This was agreed and the contract was duly amended, but throughout 1986 final approval was withheld.

Even in the early months of 1987, Mike Kimberley had not yet approved the new deal, despite the fact that everything seemed to be satisfactory to all parties. Graham Nearn was still keen to produce new cylinder heads, and had every intention of doing so, one day.

The danger was that, before long, 'unofficial' cylinder heads might appear—a British legal case between Unipart and Armstrong Patents, resulting in victory for Armstrong, has set a precedent which means that Lotus (or Graham Nearn) would be powerless to prevent this happening. As a long-established Lotus dealer, and now a manufacturer in his own right, Graham Nearn understands the urgent need for genuine-specification heads, and is doing his utmost to make this possible. At the time of writing, advance orders for these heads run into hundreds, and, at 1987 prices, the likely cost for a studded-up head would be around £1500. However, as time passes, that cost will rise.

NOTE The cylinder heads are now being re-manufactured under a joint agreement between Caterham Car Sales and Fibreglass Services, although in early 1988 the original contract remained, unsigned, at Lotus.

With hindsight, should Lotus have continued to produce these items? After all, the fibreglass bodies never rust away, and it is a relatively easy job to fit new chassis to the twin-cam engined cars. If engines continue to remain available, these Lotus cars should be around for many years after their rival cars have rusted away. One can speculate that if Lotus had always had a firm financial background, these parts would have been available—and, if so, many specialists and spurious suppliers would never have been established. Certainly, people like Roy Smith and Hugh Wilson always wished that this could have been the position.

6 The Lotus/Caterham Seven agreement

Under Mike Warner of Lotus Components at Hethel, the Lotus Seven S3 had a standard twin-cam engine. Later, in 1970, he collaborated with Holbay (as they were one of the 'names' of the era) to produce the S3 SS with a 'tweaked' twin-cam giving 125 or 135 bhp. Only 13 of these cars were made, and with the announcement of the Big Valve unit, at 126 bhp, the Holbay tuned version was dropped. Following on from the S3 came the Seven S4, in either Big Valve form—which gave 0–60 in 6.5 seconds and a top speed of around 115 mph—or with the 1600 GT Cortina pushrod engine.

Unfortunately, Mike Warner then had a disagreement with Colin Chapman and left; soon afterwards, Lotus Components closed down (in 1971) after a successful run of building all types of racing, sports and the Seven cars. Finally, all Seven production was terminated at Hethel, and eventually Graham Nearn was awarded the sole manufacturing rights in April 1973.

The S4 continued for a year at Caterham until it was dropped in favour of the 'real' Seven, the S3. Initially, the Caterham S3 was only offered with the twin-cam engine, which was still being bought outright from Hethel. The contract between Lotus and Caterham, stated that the former would continue to supply engines. This held good until 1976, when the supply of heads stopped because Lotus were unable to machine them due to production overloading on the 2 litre type 907 series of engines, and because the equipment was becoming old. Alas, the twin-cam crankshafts were becoming scarce as well.

At this time, Vegantune were having crank-shafts machined from a forging and had machining facilities for the head, so David Wakefield bought a Lotus kit from Hethel, which included the unmachined head (still from William Mills), block and all the insides. Vegantune machined the head and assembled it, supplied the crankshaft, built the entire engine and returned it to Caterham—this started in 1977. On 1 March 1978, Lotus appointed Vegantune as official twin-cam reconditioners, partly to honour the Caterham Car Sales agreement.

At this point, William Mills was taken over by Birmid (the original head casters) and produced approximately 50 heads for Caterham, which were machined and assembled during 1979. The Birmid foundry was then used for other purposes, which meant that cylinder heads were no longer available. Birmid insisted that the twin-cam engine pattern equipment was removed by the Lotus factory, as they were not willing to release it to any other company. Therefore, Lotus repossessed it.

Consequently, Caterham had supply problems, with no cylinder heads, so Lotus agreed to lend the pattern equipment to Vegantune, for that company to manufacture heads. Vegantune tried two foundries—Destec and Ingamells at Lincoln. Unfortunately, the reject rate was very high, for Ingamells was unable to cope; some heads were so porous that water leaked out everywhere.

Once again, Caterham found itself in trouble. Therefore, Vegantune resin-impregnated the heads (at Industrial Impregnation of Worley, in Worcestershire) in a process which forced resin into the head under pressure, sealing any cracks or blow-holes. Unfortunately, some of the heads were then heat treated, which totally destroyed the resin treatment.

The result was that engines were still not available—Vegantune told Caterham that there were problems with the heads, while Ingamells

Left
One of the 13 Holbay twin-cam powered Seven S3s, built by Lotus Components in 1970

Below left
The Holbay twin-cam engine as fitted to the Lotus Seven S3. This engine produced 135 bhp

Below
A Big Valve engine tucked snugly into the Caterham Seven S3. It gave very rapid acceleration, with 0-60 mph possible in just over six seconds

assured them that their bills had not been paid! Next, Ingamells went into liquidation, and Lotus repossessed the pattern equipment in 1980. In the summer of that year, Lotus terminated Vegantune's contract, following pressure from a neighbouring Lotus dealer, apparently because Vegantune was assuming 'dealer' status and purchasing many components other than engine parts from Lotus. There had also been many problems concerning the standard of reconditioning, which had been relayed to the Lotus service department. As a result, Caterham witnessed the collapse of the twin-cam project, and for the Super Seven reverted to the use of the pushrod 1.6 litre Ford Cortina engine.

The situation then became even more complicated, for Vegantune introduced its own Ford-based VTA engine, which was built on the 1.6 litre 'Kent' block, and for which 130 bhp was claimed. This had a new cylinder head design (cast at South Links Patterns and machined at Vegantune), which featured different porting, valves, and belt-driven rather than chain-driven camshafts. The standard Lotus crankshaft and rods were used, but with Vegantune pistons.

The Vegantune engines were supplied to Caterham, who built about 40 VTA-Super Sevens before Vegantune suffered another financial crisis. Between May 1984 and the beginning of 1985, only three engines were supplied—against orders of 30 units—and eventually Caterham abandoned the project, retrieved its own equipment, and substituted Cosworth BDR, or Ford pushrod engines.

Vegantune, incidentally, was founded by George Robinson and John Sisme in 1964; originally, George had been a metal fabricator at BRM, and is well known to Tony Rudd. At first, Vegantune assembled twin-cam engines on the basis of blocks and heads acquired from Lotus at Cheshunt, and by modifying BRM Phase IV camshafts to produce its 'own-brand' V5 profile. Eventually, the company came to offer a range of tune-up kits, not unlike those of BRM, and in 1966 it was supplying Ford at Boreham (rally engines) and Alan Mann Racing. The last engine for Alan Mann was supplied in 1969, complete with Lucas fuel injection, a 12.0:1 compression ratio—and 185 bhp.

Vegantune also supplied Formula B twin-cam

Above
Vegantune built works rally engines for Ford in 1967. This example had Lucas fuel injection and was dry-sumped

Left
This was Vegantune's project to provide a 16-valve cylinder head for the twin-cam engine. Only one casting was ever made, and the idea was never developed

engines to the USA until 1973, by which time John Sisme had left the company. Among other Vegantune twin-cam engines was an 1100 cc version for the American SCCA Formula C of 1967. This had an 80.9 mm cylinder bore, a short stroke, Weber 45 DCOE carbs, and produced more than 100 bhp at 10,400 rpm; 15 were produced with a standard camshaft chain, but with an extra damper on the cam cover above the sprockets, and another below the chain tensioner. There was also a 1300 cc unit for American C-Sports racing, with an 82.5 mm bore and short stroke, which produced 154 bhp at 9250 rpm; 25 of these engines were built. Only one Vegantune 997 cc twin-cam was ever made, and there was

only one four-valve twin-cam head, for there was never enough money available to develop these engines further.

Vegantune suffered a series of financial crises, and is now known as Vegantune/Evante Cars Ltd. Under this name, the company has begun producing a Lotus Elan look-alike called the Evante.

The only other official twin-cam engine reconditioner was Ian Walker who, under the banner of Ian Walker Racing, was involved in racing Lotus 11s, and then his famous Elite, registered EL5. This won 14 races in a year with Mike Costin looking after it, and was followed by a 26R and his Lotus-Cortinas driven by the likes of Paul Hawkins, Frank Gardner, Mike Spence and the Lotus works drivers Peter Arundell, Jim Clark and Trevor Taylor. However, he stopped racing in 1964.

Ian also designed an Elan-based car for Le Mans, which Jackie Stewart and Mike Spence drove. He then went into the tuning business in North Finchley, offering four stages of tune on the engines. He built up a reconditioning service and eventually a stock, for resale or exchange, which ranged from the standard 105 bhp tune to full-race tune. Because of his friendship with Colin Chapman, he asked if this was acceptable, and the result was that he became an official reconditioner in 1971, as well as a service agent. In 1977 he stopped this, because of the high cost of engine parts, and went into the parts-supply business, eventually starting his now highly-successful Blue Flash company, which supplies component parts to the motor industry. His engines were on a par with the Mike Spence Elans of 1967, and although it is not as highly sought after as the Mike Spence BRM Elan, nonetheless the genuine IWR engine is a bonus to buyers today.

Above
A Lotus Seven S3 with Novomotor-prepared twin-cam engine, reputed to push out around 170 bhp!

Above left
Vegantune also produced a turbocharged version of the twin-cam engine in 1976. Only two such units were built, but they were not successful. As shown, complete with Garrett turbocharger and an 8.0:1 compression ratio, the engine was claimed to produce 200 bhp

Overleaf
Three tests of IWR-converted, twin-cam engined cars—all highly complimentary of this company's work on the unit

0 - 100 m.p.h. in 17.0 secs.

THE IAN WALKER LOTUS ELAN

THERE are several ways of improving acceleration, such as tuning the engine or lowering the final drive ratio. When both are combined on the same car the results are often sensational. Such is the case with the Stage 3 Ian Walker-tuned Coupé Lotus Elan, which will accelerate from 0-60 m.p.h. in 6.8 seconds, to 80 m.p.h. in 11 seconds, 100 m.p.h. in 17.0 seconds, and streak over the standing quarter mile in 15½ seconds.

This is achieved by combining Ian Walker's 135 b.h.p. conversion with a 4.4:1 axle ratio. The conversion, costing £146, and the axle £35. The tuning part may seem expensive, but this includes a virtually complete strip down and rebuild of the standard engine with balancing of the crankshaft, flywheel and clutch assembly as well as connecting rods and pistons.

The cylinder head is fully modified with improvements made to combustion chamber and inlet tract shape, and two new camshafts are supplied and fitted. A modified timing chain tensioner is fitted, different main and big-end bearing shells are supplied, and the oil pressure relief valve is changed. The engine is then built up and given an electronic tune-up.

Of almost as much interest to us as the tuning components, was the Elan itself, for we have not yet driven a standard Elan coupé. This makes it impossible to give comparative acceleration figures, which would be rather pointless anyway due to the low axle of the Walker car.

The first impression when driving the coupé, even with the more powerful engine, is the much lower noise level compared with the open model. Engine and gearbox noise is much reduced and the radio could be heard at 80 m.p.h., an impossible feat in the open model.

The standard of interior finish and trim is much improved, and the electric windows work silently and smoothly. Lotus have obviously learned much with the S1 and S2 open models, making the coupé a very sophisticated car.

Naturally, with the power output and low axle ratio the Walker car accelerated like a rocket, as the data panel shows. The Elan is not the best car at getting away from a standstill due to the elasticity in the rubber doughnuts, but the Walker car streaked away very cleanly with little wind-up at all. Of course, with the low final drive the car reached 7,000 r.p.m. in

the gears very quickly, the speeds gears very quickly, the speeds in the three lower gears being 43, 65 and 85 m.p.h. Top speed is just on 105 m.p.h. at 7,000 r.p.m., but the engine sounds distinctly fussy at this speed, and one has the feeling that there should be another gear. The normal owner will obviously prefer a higher ratio as on long, straight roads the engine is screaming its head off, although it really comes into its own on twisty roads where it can be flung around as only an Elan can.

Certainly nothing, *but nothing*, can stay with the Walker Elan on roads which are anything but straight, the handling, acceleration and braking being out of this world.

The Elan must be one of the world's best sports cars, and this Walker version transforms the low-speed acceleration into the near-E-type class. Now if only Colin Chapman could drop in a ZF five-speed box we might be nearly there!

M.L.T.

POKE: The Ian Walker mods, costing £146, give the twin-cam Lotus engine 135 b.h.p. and will accelerate a 4.4:1 axled Elan over the quarter mile in 15½ seconds.

MOTORING NEWS TUNING TEST

Performance		Speeds in the gears	
0-30 m.p.h.	2.5 secs.	First	43 m.p.h.
0-40 m.p.h.	3.5 secs.	Second	65 m.p.h.
0-50 m.p.h.	5.6 secs.	Third	85 m.p.h.
0-60 m.p.h.	6.8 secs.	Top	105 m.p.h.
0-70 m.p.h.	9.0 secs.		
0-80 m.p.h.	11.0 secs.		
0-90 m.p.h.	14.0 secs.		
0-100 m.p.h.	17.0 secs.		
Standing start ¼-mile			
	15.5 secs.		

Conversion by Ian Walker Ltd., 236 Woodhouse Road, London, N.12.

SLEEK: The coupé Elan is a much more sophisticated car than the open version, as both wind and engine noise are greatly reduced.

Reprinted from 15th October 1966 issue of *Motoring News*

Reprinted from **sportscar** *March issue 1966*

'Off the shelf' Lotus Cortinas can be reckoned to accelerate from 0 to 50 mph in just under 8 seconds and reach a top speed of between 105 and 110 mph. Now this is good enough for a lot of people, but not quite good enough for some, which is where Ian Walker has stepped in.

From new premises at 236 Woodhouse Road, London N12, Ian Walker Ltd are marketing a series of four conversions for this model, aimed at more performance, better handling, and improved reliability. There are three engine conversions, Stage 1 being an exchange camshafts job, Stage 2 a cylinder head exchange, and Stage 3 a combination of these two, plus bottom-end modifications and balancing. The fourth conversion is for 'A' bracket rear suspension cars, and converts them to current leafspring specification.

The car supplied for test had the Stage 3 engine conversion plus the rear-end conversion, representing an investment, in all, of £190. Of this, £50 goes on the suspension equipment and labour charge. The kit of parts includes a one-piece prop shaft, leaf springs (which are lowered by 1¼ inches) and new pinion flange, as well as Armstrong Firmaride dampers. Adjustarides can be specified for an extra £2 10s, or Selectarides for an extra £7 10s.

The Firmarides on the test car seemed to give just the right amount of ride stiffness for low-speed comfort, but their value was even more appreciated during high-speed cornering over an inferior surface. Despite the lack of anti-tramp bars, there was little evidence of wheel hop, and in the breakaway state the back wheels tended merely to drag their tyres (Cinturato 165s) rather than to develop a slide.

But of course, apart from any improvement in handling which may result, the real value of this conversion is that it removes one of the main hazards of ownership of a coil-sprung

Lotus Cortina, namely rear axle failure, caused by the inability of the differential housing to withstand the loads transferred to it through the 'A' bracket during high-speed cornering. This in itself must be worth most of the cost of the conversion.

The Stage 3 engine job involves a pair of camshafts giving a timing of 51 BTDC, 78 ABDC, 75 BBDC and 54 ATDC, and providing a considerable power boost above 3,000 rpm. Valve lift is .350 inch, and standard tappet clearances are used. Inevitably, some low-speed flexibility is sacrificed, but this is retrieved by the modifications to the head, and in particular to the opening out and straightening of the inlet ports. The head is shaved 20 thou, giving half a ratio increase of compression. At the same time, the distributor cut-out is removed, and modified timing chain tensioner, big-end and main bearing shells, oil pressure relief valve and felt filter fitted. In view of the higher revs obtainable, the whole unit is carefully balanced, and finally is re-jetted to suit customers' individual requirements.

'Our' Lotus Cortina was, in fact, a customer's car, and had covered several thousands of miles since conversion. It was not tuned up in any way for the test, just given a hose down and handed over. It represented, therefore, the sort of performance which the IWR conversion can be expected to give during normal day-by-day running after settling down from its initial condition of peak tune.

Three things immediately were apparent. First, the extra power, especially over 4,000 rpm. Second, the improved flexibility low down. Third, the lack of any noticeable increase in noise level.

On the power side, the performance improvement inevitably helped acceleration times at the top end, but throughout the range there was a reasonable improvement on the figures which might be expected from a standard car in prime condition. The smoothness of the unit between 5,000 and 7,000 rpm was eloquent of the care with which the unit had been balanced, although in the indirect gears there was no point at all in exceeding 6,000 rpm.

The bottom-end flexibility allowed the car to accelerate smoothly in top gear from 1,700 rpm, and from as low as 1,100 rpm on level ground provided the accelerator was treated very gently. A fairly sharp opening of the throttles at low to medium engine speeds could produce immediate response followed by a second or so of hesitation, suggestive of partial fuel starvation. The crankshaft speed at which the hesitation occurred could be varied between under 2,000 and around 4,000 rpm according to the gear and the amount of throttle used.

The low noise level was highly commendable, as indeed was the overall fuel consumption which, at 22 mpg, was as good as one might reasonably expect from the standard car, which turns out some 105 bhp compared with approximately 135 from the Walker version.

BETTER BOTH ENDS

A Lotus Cortina with the IWR treatment

The following acceleration times were recorded in slightly less than ideal conditions:		
	0-30 mph	3.2 seconds
	0-40 mph	4.8 seconds
	0-50 mph	6.8 seconds
	0-60 mph	9.2 seconds
	0-70 mph	12.4 seconds
	0-80 mph	15.8 seconds
	0-90 mph	20.4 seconds
	Top speed (at 7,000 rpm) 122 mph.	

THE IWR LOTUS ELAN COUPÉ

Road Test by John Bolster

TO drive fast cars effectively is no longer legal in England. Not only is the 70 mph limit still with us, but there are now dark rumours of an eventual 60 mph maximum. Strikes permitting, one shakes the dust of this ill-governed land off one's wheels and heads for civilization.

The annual trip to Le Mans gives an opportunity to extend a really fast car continuously. With fast roads, but lots of bumps and corners, there is plenty of variety, and the circuit itself has all the necessary distances marked out for performance testing on the Mulsanne straight. I get up at 4 am to ensure that the road will be clear, for by that time the last of the customers have zig-zagged away from the *Café de l'Hippodrome*, though the early morning mist is troublesome.

For such a journey one needs a real car, and I was delighted when Ian Walker offered me an Elan Coupé. He has a standard conversion service for this model, producing a greatly improved version at a remarkably moderate price. The backbone chassis with all-independent suspension remains standard, for who could improve that? The four-wheel disc brakes gain a servo and the engine is completely rebuilt to develop 138 bhp continuously.

Two special camshafts are fitted to a modified cylinder head, which gives a compression ratio of 11 to 1 instead of the normal 9.5 to 1. The ports and combustion chambers are worked upon while the two twin-choke Weber carburetters are reset. To cope with the increased engine speed, the moving parts are dynamically balanced and a bigger oil pump looks after the special racing-type bearing shells. The timing-chain tensioner is also beefed-up.

The very pleasant coupé body, with its electrically operated windows and mahogany instrument panel, is refinished in polychromatic royal blue, to coachbuilders' standards. A small leather-rim steering wheel is fitted and the lamps are of the Cibié assymetric high-speed type.

Normally, the Elan has a 3.9 to 1 final drive ratio, which works well in England but does not permit 110 mph cruising on the Continent. An alternative 3.55 to 1 gear is available, and this was fitted to the test car. It is normal to change the gearbox for one with rather wider ratios when this gear end is installed. However, the Elan I used had both the "high" final drive and the close-ratio box.

With this gearing, it was possible to exceed 50 mph quite easily in first gear, with over 75 mph and 100 mph on second and third. This caused no trouble in the thickest Paris traffic, the flexibility of the engine being quite remarkable. Indeed, I can honestly say that I did not notice the high bottom gear, even when restarting on steep gradients.

For fast road work, these gear ratios are ideal. To obtain performance figures, however, a much lower bottom gear (of higher numerical ratio) would be desirable. Under these conditions, the wheels spin for a moment and then the engine "fluffs" before really taking hold. The acceleration figures, and particularly that for the standing quarter-mile, are not in any way representative of the real performance of the car. With wider ratios, a 14.5 sec quarter-mile should be possible. The real answer, of course, would be a five-speed box, but this is not available at present, so I hope to test an IWR Elan shortly with low gearing to suit English conditions and give violent acceleration.

The maximum speed depends entirely on how far into the red you are willing to let the rev-counter go. I timed the car at a genuine 130 mph after quite a short run, but the hand was then well past the 7000 possible after a longer run, but I did not wish to over-stress the engine and called it a day. Much more valuable is the machine's ability to attain 120 mph incredibly quickly.

All this performance is usable because the exhaust is remarkably quiet. Nowadays, the man who drives with a "rorty" exhaust is asking for trouble, and I was delighted to be able to use the full acceleration in Paris without attracting the attention of the *flics*. The ride is comfortable over all but the worst roads of northern France and the driving position is ideal. Personally, I would prefer a slightly larger steering wheel, but then I am probably old-fashioned.

The Elan is famous for its cornering and controllability. If you have a preference for any special handling characteristic, you can get it by altering the tyre pressures to suit your whim. It is difficult to analyse exactly what is so good about the Elan's roadholding. Perhaps one could say that it is like the better front-wheel-drive

THE usual smooth lines of the Elan are not tampered with on the IWR car (above). Just to the right the upturned lid reveals plentiful sound-proofing and in the foreground are the two twin-choke Webers with a vacuum pipe to the servo.

machines, but that it retains the extra controllability which variation of power on the rear tyres provides.

The balanced engine is smooth at all speeds within its range. It is not mechanically noisy and never tends to oil a plug in the worst traffic, though it does consume a modicum of lubricant, as an occasional blue puff from the exhaust confirms. In one of those early evening jams for which the Boulevard St Michel is infamous, the water temperature did tend to soar, and I switched off the ignition when the opportunity offered itself. However, I know that a standard Elan would have been similarly affected.

The fuel economy was astonishing. Using 6000 rpm in the gears and cruising always at over 100 mph, I averaged 27 mpg. Whether this was partly due to the French roads I cannot say, but it is a remarkable result for an engine with one carburetter choke for each cylinder.

The Elan is a wonderfully safe car, for it has fierce acceleration and powerful fade-free brakes, while that reserve of roadholding is always there to cope with sudden emergencies. It does not become so hot in the interior as most front-engined, rear-drive coupés do—and I drove it across France in a heat wave. It is also completely

water-tight in a cloudburst, whereas most British cars leak like sieves under such conditions.

My conclusion is that I certainly chose the right car for the 1966 Le Mans trip. The 138 bhp engine is just as tractable as the standard one and it is completely reliable because it is specifically built for increased performance from the bottom end up. For further details, contact Ian Walker, Ltd., at Woodhouse Service Station, 236 Woodhouse Road, N.12.

SPECIFICATION AND PERFORMANCE DATA

Car Tested: IWR Lotus Elan Coupé, price £1,527 in component form or £1,559 assembled for export.

Engine: Four-cylinders 82.55 mm x 72.75 mm (1558 cc). Twin chain-driven overhead camshafts. Compression ratio 11 to 1. 138 bhp at 6500 rpm. Two twin-choke Weber carburetters. Lucas coil and distributor.

Transmission: Single dry plate clutch. Four-speed all-synchromesh gearbox, ratios 1, 1.23, 1.636 and 2.51 to 1. Chassis-mounted hypoid final drive unit, ratio 3.55 to 1.

Chassis: Steel central backbone chassis. Independent front suspension by wishbones and helical springs. Rack and pinion steering. Independent rear suspension by bottom wishbones and struts with helical springs. Telescopic dampers all round. Disc brakes front and rear with servo assistance. Centre-locking disc wheels with three-eared caps, fitted 145 x 13 SP tyres.

Graph:

MAX. SPEED 130 M.P.H.

¼ MILE

IWR LOTUS ELAN

M.P.H. (vertical axis, 0 to 120)
SECONDS (horizontal axis, 0 to 24)

ACCELERATION GRAPH

Equipment: 12-volt lighting and starting. Speedometer. Rev counter. Ammeter. Oil pressure, water temperature, and fuel gauges. Heating and demisting. Variable speed windscreen wipers and washers. Electrically controlled windows. Flashing direction indicators. Radio (extra).

Dimensions: Wheelbase 7 ft. Track 4 ft. Overall length 12 ft 1¼ ins. Width 4 ft 8 ins. Turning circle 29 ft 9 ins. Weight 13 cwt (dry).

Performance: Maximum speed 130 mph. Speeds in gears: 3rd 100 mph, 2nd 75 mph, 1st 50 mph. Standing quarter-mile 16 secs. Acceleration: 0-30 mph, 3.6 secs; 0-60 mph, 7.6 secs; 0-80 mph, 13.2 secs; 0-100 mph, 18.4 secs.

Fuel Consumption: 27 mpg.

7 Other cars and oddities

The twin-cam engine did not find its way into many different cars, other than Lotus and Ford models. The reason is hard to define, but perhaps Colin Chapman did not sanction the release of his engine to others he felt would not enhance its reputation, or perhaps the cost was too high for other small builders to accept, or maybe no one wanted it! Certainly, no TVR or Marcos production car ever enjoyed the use of the twin-cam engine.

The Elva Mk 7S and the Sebring Courier were offered with a choice of engines, the twin-cam being one of them. Elva used the engine as early as January 1963, and continued until 1964, when the BMW 1600 took over as the favourite unit. Ginetta used it with success, in the G4s and G12s, while David Lazenby, the Lotus Formula 1 mechanic, put a twin-cam in an Elite he assembled in 1967. This caused a mild ripple in the motoring press at the time, for they called it a rebirth of the Elite. The Costin Nathan (designed by Frank Costin) had a twin-cam in it. In America the Bobsey—a two-seat, all-alloy-panelled car—had a twin-cam, and Lee Grand also produced a car with a twin-cam, but the numbers were small.

Many privateers fitted twin-cams into just about everything, including Minis, Fiat 500s, and lawn mowers! Also three twin-cylinder twin-cams were made by a Vegantune mechanic, who cut the engines in half. They were installed in a racing motorcycle and sidecar, and they survived!

What followed the engine? The Cosworth BDA was built alongside the twin-cam and, after the original twin-cam blocks had disappeared, the 1600 cc unit used the 1600 Kent block with the GT crankshaft and rods, but with Lotus pistons. The block face was machined down by approximately 0.250 in. and an alloy front-cover spacer plate was fitted to restore the correct height. The camshaft drive chain was lengthened by two links, and the tensioner pivot bracket was extended so that the correct chain tension could be maintained. The engine's overall height was increased by between $\frac{1}{4}$ and $\frac{3}{8}$ in. Consequently, the power output could be raised, and the engine could be enlarged to 1.8 litres. Needless to say, the Lotus factory did not approve of this project, in any way.

What of the rivals? Alfa Romeo's twin-cam unit is still with us, as is the Fiat twin-cam, but in the late 1980s it is Toyota who build some of the best twin-cam engines, as (for instance) fitted to the MR2 sports car. This engine was originally intended for the new small Lotus (M90, later coded X100), in 1.6 litre or 2 litre form. However, after many delays, the X100 may now have an entirely different engine by the time it appears (in 1989, or even later?).

Certainly, the MR2 has filled the gap left by the much-loved Elan. The Toyota unit may not have the same sporting heritage as the Lotus twin-cam, but it will surely become a classic in the future, just as the Lotus twin-cam is now.

Without a doubt, the Lotus twin-cam was one of the most successful engines of all time.

Above right
The racing Lotus 23B's engine, showing the oil tank for the dry sump, and the cam-cover oil pipe, which has been blocked off and filled in. Oil vent pipes from the tank and engine lead to the oil catch tank

Right
The Elva Sebring Courier was built by Trojan-Elva, and first displayed at the 1964 Racing Car Show. One of the various engines on offer was a 140 bhp, Cosworth-tuned, Lotus twin-cam

Above left
Allan Miles driving his twin-cam engined Sebring
Courier at Brands Hatch in a 1980s event

Left
This is the engine bay of Allan Miles' Elva Sebring
Courier. The shot was taken in 1986, but the car
dates from 1964 and has been beautifully preserved

Above
Mike Harrison driving an Elva Mk 7S at Thruxton
on 7 May 1979, in a ten-lap historic race. Result:
eighth overall, with power by Lotus twin-cam

Above
This 1986 photo shows the engine bay of the
mid-engined Elva Mk 7; this car was originally built
in 1963

Above right and right
A full-race, dry-sump twin-cam engine powers this
Ginetta G12

The ex-David Lazenby twin-cam Elite, registered MPW 804E, which is now owned by Brian Stutz in Switzerland. The engine is a standard 105 bhp unit, mated to a close-ratio Lotus-Cortina gearbox. The pedals were moved to the floor to allow the Weber carburettors to fit into the engine bay, and the wiper motor was moved to the other side of the car. The radiator used is from a normal Elite. Uprated front springs were required to cope with the increased weight of the engine, compared with the usual Coventry Climax unit. The exterior is pure Elite and gives no clue to the special engine being used

Above
The Ford-Cosworth BDA engine in an Escort—this powerplant replaced the Lotus twin-cam unit

Above left and left
A Turner car, fitted with a standard Lotus twin-cam engine

Right
A twin-cam built on a 1600 block, showing the alloy spacer plate between the head and the front cover

8 Production details

Regrettably, Lotus did not keep any records of the number of engines made in standard, S/E and Big Valve form, or of the engines using Stromberg instead of Weber or Dellorto carburettors. No records exist of how many Federal or European emission types were made. The only records covering the period up to 1970 are kept in the old fire-station hut at Hethel and record the chassis number, the engine number and the date invoiced. Only from 1970, when records changed to the modern system, can the engine be ascribed to a specific car.

The total production figure quoted is a fairly accurate guess by Lotus and Ford, but the discrepancy in the last unit produced at Hethel is because some engines 'went for a walk', some were duplicated and a few were sold as kits to Caterham Car Sales (approximately 50) to honour the Lotus/Caterham Seven agreement. Some of the last engines were placed in Europas and +2S130/5s that were hastily built in 1975 (registered into 1976, English 'P' plate) in an effort to salvage some money after the disastrous launch, in 1974, of the Elite (Type 75) which was not selling at all well and was financially embarrassing to Lotus. Indeed, at the time, there was no money available to build the first Esprits (Type 79), so this was delayed until July 1976, after its first appearance at Earls Court in October 1975.

Twin-cam production
Total units produced: approximately 34,000
Last numbered unit produced at Hethel in 1975: 32,600
(Fitted in a Europa Twin-Cam Special painted silver for Mr P. Hunt)
Last listed unit in the end sequence: 32,537
(Fitted in last-of-the-line Europa Special)

No one can reconcile the last two figures—what happened to 63 other engines if, indeed, they existed, or did Mr Hunt (a Lotus employee) request a round figure to end on? 32,600 certainly exists. The engines used in the last batch of Europas and +2S130/5s were presumably included in the 32,537 total; if not, 63 other cars were certainly not built. Indeed, Lotus do not know how many extra cars were made! This vagueness is typical of the company, and its historical records.

NOTE Engine number 25,000 was presented to Walter Hayes at the 1970 Earls Court Motor Show.
Total number of 1498 cc engines produced was only 11—six of them went into 23s, the other five into the Elan 1500 models.
Official debut: Nürburgring 1000 km race, May 1962 (1498 cc).
Official launch: Earls Court Motor Show, October 1962 (1498 cc).
Official Big Valve launch: Earls Court Motor Show, October 1970.

Production changes
L-type rods disappeared, replaced by C-type in late 1963/early 1964.
Tappet sleeves fitted from mid-1964 at engine number 1576.
Four-bolt crankshaft and A-type pistons used up to engine number 7799.
Six-bolt crankshaft, revised rear seal and C-type pistons, used from mid-1967, from engine number 7800.
Exhaust-valve material changed, requiring different tappet clearances (0.009–0.011 in.), during 1967, from engine number 9952.
Spigot bearing changed to needle-roller type, 1969, from engine number 18,500.

Non-shouldered head bolts (stronger than original type) introduced in 1969, from engine number 18,820.

Renewable oil-filter canister on new oil pump introduced in late 1970, from engine number 23,607.

Apart from gasket sealant and material specifications, no other running changes were made, which is quite remarkable considering the length of the engine's career. The two main changes were the introduction of the Stromberg head, in March 1969, and the Big Valve head in October 1970.